HAWAIIAN NAMES ENGLISH NAMES

EILEEN M. ROOT

HAWAIIAN NAMES ENGLISH NAMES

PRESS PACIFICA

Library of Congress Cataloging-in-Publication Data

Root, Eileen M.
   Hawaiian names—English names.

   Includes bibliographical references.
   1. Names, Personal—Hawaiian.   2. Names—Hawaii.
I. Title.
CS2377.R66   1876   929.4'089994   87-29133
ISBN 0-916630-62-5

BOOK INQUIRIES AND ORDERS:
Booklines Hawaii, Ltd.
269 Palii Street
Mililani, Hawaii 96789
Phone: (808) 676-0116

Printed in the UNITED STATES OF AMERICA

Cover design by Pam Castaldi

Typesetting by:
The Last Word, Kailua, HI 96734

Manufactured by:

  RR Donnelley, Menasha, WI

ACKNOWLEDGEMENTS

In his preface to Hawaiian Grammar in 1979 Samuel H. Elbert noted that he had been studying the Hawaiian language for 40 years, and that co-author Mary Kawena Pukui had been studying the Hawaiian language for 80 years. Samuel H. Elbert's and Mary Kawena Pukui's combined 120 years of devotion to the Hawaiian language and the books they have written over the years, especially the Hawaiian Dictionary, have made this book on one very small but fascinating aspect of the Hawaiian language and culture possible.

The State of Hawai'i Library System provided both encouragement and support for this project through a sabbatical leave. The Kāne'ohe Regional Library; the Hawai'i State Library, Hawaiian and Pacific and Collection; the University of Hawai'i Library, Hawaiian/Pacific Collection; and the Midkiff Learning Center at Kamehameha Schools all provided resource materials, and that most valuable resource of all, the knowledge and enthusiasm of their staffs.

Carol Silva of the Hawaii State Archives provided valuable advice and assistance. Elynore Hambleton assisted with the tedious proof-reading.

Alex Lichton first alerted the publisher to the need of a book of Hawaiian and English names as a result of the queries he received during his tenure in a Hawai'i bookstore; thus, he was instrumental in getting the publisher interested in this project. The need is now fulfilled with "Hawaiian Names, English Names."

CONTENTS

About Names
and Naming in Old Hawai'i

Today most people choose a name because "it sounds nice". In ancient Hawai'i, and indeed, in most traditional societies, a name involved more than its sound.

A name (inoa) was a possession, an influence for good or evil, and perhaps a part of a society's history. One's inoa was a precious personal possession and also a force in its own right. Although a person possessed his or her name, he or she was also possessed by the name. Once spoken, the inoa assumed a mystical existence and the power to help or harm the bearer. And, so went the belief, the more a name was spoken, the more powerful it became, and the more powerful its influence—good or evil.

Therefore, the choice of the inoa was a very important event. The naming of a new-born would involve the extended family ('ohana) and, ideally, the supernatural advice of the family ancestor god ('aumakua).

Names suggested by supernatural forces were the inoa pō—literally night name or dream name; the inoa hō'ailona—the name in a sign; and the inoa 'ūlāleo—the name heard in a mystical voice. Prior to the birth of a child, a member of the family might have a name revealed in one of these ways.

It was believed that any name provided by the ancestor god must be used. To ignore this name would bring illness, and eventually death to the child. Mary Kawena Pukui, co-author of the Hawaiian dictionary, tells the story behind her Hawaiian name:

"Some 78 years ago, a baby girl was born on the island of Hawaii. Shortly after the birth, an aunt was given an inoa pō for the child. But because she had become a Christian, the aunt kept the name a secret and the child was not given the mystically-indicated inoa. The little girl soon became ill. The family held an ho'oponopono (the formal gathering of all family members for mutual confession of wrongs, forgiveness, and restoration of good relationships), during which the aunt told about the inoa pō. Clearly, the family agreed, an offended 'aumakua was making the child sick. And so after a mōhai (sacrificial offering, in this case food), a feast, and many prayers, the old name was 'oki'd (severed or removed) and the child was given the inoa pō.

And forthwith Kawena-'ula-o-kalani-a-Hi'iaka-i-ka-poli-o-Pele-ka-wahine-'ai-honua ("The rosy glow in the sky made by Hi'iaka, reared in the bosom of Pele, the earth-consuming woman") recovered and grew up to be Mary Kawena Pukui. . ."*

A name, once given, became the property of the owner, not to be taken by another without permission. To steal another's name was kapu—to violate this kapu would bring illness or bad fortune.

In ancient times, the ali'i would often have several different names. As 'of the gods' the ali'i were considered sacred and would have a sacred name. This name often expressed a degree of rank and was a key to the bearer's genealogy. This sacred name was never used in public, so the ali'i would also have a public or familiar name. In addition, an ali'i might acquire a popular name, similar to a nickname, and yet more names given in commemoration of events or achievements.

According to ancient Hawaiian custom, these sacred or secret names were forbidden to those outside the family. Only a member of the family—a person who had a right to the sacred name—could give that name.

Other types of names used in ancient Hawai'i were inoa kapuna—ancestral names, and inoa ho'omanao—commemorative names recalling a special person, place, or event.

Two special types of names that today seem very strange to us are the inoa kuāmuamu—the reviling name and the resentment name. A reviling name was given to trick an evil spirit. Illness might be a sign that a child was possessed by an evil spirit. If the child was named something unpleasant or even loathsome, the evil spirit might be disgusted, and stay away!

2

A resentment name was like a commemorative name, but the event it recalled was the occasion of a hurt or insult.

Since a name could influence a person's whole life, health, and happiness, it was possible to sever ('oki) a name that violated a kapu or to change a reviling name once the need for such a name was past. The traditional ceremony would involve offerings of prayers and foods to the gods. The prayer was called the pule ho'onoa—prayer to free.

With the abolition of the kapus in 1819 and the arrival of the first Christian missionaries the following year, the traditional practices of Hawaiian naming changed drastically.

To the ancient Hawaiians a name was not necessarily a single word, nor was there a system of marriage and family names. In the 1820's, as the Hawaiians began to adopt the Christian religion, they also began to use Christian first names and their Hawaiian names (or a shortened form) frequently became last names. In 1860 Ka-mehameha IV signed The Act to Regulate Names. This act decreed that citizens of the Hawaiian Kingdom follow standard European naming practices. Women, at marriage, would acquire their husband's family name. Children would have their father's surname. And all children were required to have a Christian given name.

A Christian name usually meant a Biblical name. Many children were given both an official Christian name and a traditional Hawaiian name. In 1967 The Act to Regulate Names was changed, and the requirement that the given name be Christian was dropped. This change gave belated recognition to the cosmopolitan nature of Hawai'i's population, making it possible to use Hawaiian, Polynesian, Oriental, or any other non-Christian name as a child's official given name.

Today parents in Hawai'i have a wonderful and varied choice of names. But there is still something very special about a Hawaiian name. Even in our modern society it is possible to share in some of the ancient Hawaiian inoa beliefs. By carefully considering and understanding the Hawaiian names we choose for our children (or ourselves), we can perhaps help to perpetuate and propagate the language and culture of Hawai'i, thus enriching the future for all.

Pukui, Mary Kawena. Nānā I Ke Kumu (Look to the Source), Vol. 1, p. 95-96.

2

Pronunciation Guide

The Hawaiian alphabet has twelve letters. The consonants are H, K, L, M, N, P, and W. Their sound is similar to the English sound of these same letters with one exception. Sometimes the W will change to sound like the English V. When W follows O or U it is still pronounced as W. But if W follows E or I it sounds like a V. After A or at the beginning of a word it may sound like W or V—thus, both Hawai'i and Havai'i are correct.

The Hawaiian vowels are A, E, I, O, and U. Hawaiian words frequently have many vowels. In fact, some Hawaiian words have no consonants at all.

The vowel sounds are as follows:

A, Ā	like the A in above; Ā like the A in father
E, Ē	like the E in bet; Ē like the A in tame
I, Ī	like the EE in keep
O, Ō	like the O in go
U, Ū	like the OO in moon

There are also eight vowel pairs or diphthongs. These are pronounced by quickly combining the two vowel sounds with the emphasis on the first vowel.

The vowel pairs are:

AE, AI, AO, AU
EI, EU
OI, OU

In pronouncing Hawaiian words each letter is sounded individually with the exception of the eight vowel pairs which are merged into a single sound. Many Hawaiian words have a glottal stop ('). This sign marks a break in the sound, like the pause between oh-oh in English.

To pronounce a Hawaiian word, first divide it into syllables (or stress units). Syllables will always end in a vowel.

4

A consonant marks the beginning of a new syllable. In the 1986 edition of the "Hawaiian Dictionary" a period is used to divide words into stress units (for example: hei.au). If you are not sure how to divide a word, check this edition of the "Hawaiian Dictionary".

Finally, you must know where to place the stress (or accent) on a word. In general, the stress is on the next to the last syllable of Hawaiian words. However, all long vowels (shown by a dash over the vowel called a macron) are stressed. A stressed vowel is longer and stronger—some words will have several stressed vowels.

The preceding brief and simplified guidelines will help you pronounce Hawaiian names correctly. However, the best way to understand the sound and rhythm of a language is to hear it spoken. There are several Hawaiian language learning cassette tapes available at bookstores and the public library. "The Hawaiian Language, Its Spelling and Pronunciation" by Kalena Silva and Kauanoe Kamanā is an excellent introduction to the correct pronunciation of the sounds of the Hawaiian language.

A List of Hawaiian Names

The following list of over 800 ready-made Hawaiian names has been gathered from many sources. Many Hawaiian names are composed of several words. To help you understand the individual words that compose certain names a dash is used. For example, Ke-kai-malu, the peaceful sea (ke = the, kai = sea, malu = peaceful). When you use these compound names the dash may be omitted, e.g. Kekaimalu.

Names beginning with K are the most numerous because Ka and Ke mean the. In many cases the article can be dropped without changing the meaning of the name. The translation that follows each name may not be the only possible translation. Translations have been chosen based on traditional meanings for historic and legendary names. For other names commonly accepted meanings from reliable sources have been chosen.

You should be aware that there can be several interpretations of the meaning of a single name. Words can have two or three meanings and the meaning one person chooses may differ from the meaning chosen by another person. For example, in 1973 the King and Queen of the Aloha Week Parade each had the same name—Ke-'alohi-lani. To the King's family, his name meant 'the splendor of heaven'. To the Queen's family, her name meant 'slow-moving heaven'. In our listing we give you 'the shining heaven' and 'the brightness of heaven' as meanings for this same name!

Most Hawaiian names are uni-sex, equally suitable for boys or girls. The meaning should be your guide.

This list is far from comprehensive. Since any Hawaiian word or combination of words could be a potential name, a comprehensive list would be almost endless. If you do not find a name to your liking, you may want to create your own Hawaiian name. Following the list you will find some guidelines on creating a Hawaiian name.

Two abbreviations that are used throughout the list are:

Lit., which is 'literally', or exactly, word for word
For example: Ka lei = the lei

Fig., which is 'figuratively', a figure of speech, using a certain word or words to represent another word or concept.
For example: Ka lei = sweetheart, beloved child

'A'ala	Fragrant, Fig., of high rank, royal
'A'ama-kua-lenalena	A rock crab with a yellow back, Fig., a swift, strong warrior
Ahe	Softly blowing breeze; also Aheahe
Ahuahu	Healthy, vigorous; to grow rapidly and thrive
Ahu-lani	Heavenly shrine
A'ia'i	Bright, as moonlight; fair, white, clear, pure, brilliant, shining
'Ai-lā'au	Fire god before the arrival of Pele, Lit., wood eater
'Ai-lani	One who enjoys the comforts and honors and exercises the responsibility of being a chief; also, 'Ai-ali'i, 'Ai-li'i
'Āina-kea	White land, also an especially attractive variety of sugar cane
Āiwaiwa	Inexplicable, mysterious, marvelous; wonderful because of divinity; wonderfully proficient or skilled; also notorious

---

In some names a dash is used to help you understand the individual words that compose that name. When you use the name, the dash may be omitted.

7

'Akahi   The number one in counting; an idiom meaning for the first time, never before

Akanahe   Gentle in behavior and speech

'Ākau   Right (not left), North

Akeakamai   Lover of wisdom, seeker of knowledge

'Ala   Fragrant, sweet-smelling; Fig., esteemed, chiefly. Fragrance had supernatural powers and was associated with the gods.

Alaka'i   Leader

Alamimo   Quick, nimble

Alana   Awakening

'Alaneo   Clear, serene, unclouded

Ala-ula   Light of early dawn or sunset glow, Lit., flaming road

'Ale   Wave, crest of a wave; to billow, to ripple also 'Ale'ale

'Ale-lau-loa   Wave, long and large

'Ale-po'i   Breaking waves

'Alihi kaua   Commander, one who directed in battle, strategist

Aloalo   All kinds of hibiscus including the native white hibiscus; Loved and served by many persons, as a chief or favorite child

Aloha   Love, affection, compassion, mercy, pity, kindness, charity; greetings, hello, good-by; sweetheart, loved one

Aloha-e-kau-nei   Love alighting here

'Alohi   Shining, brilliant

'Alohi-lani   Bright sky, brightness of heaven

'Ālohilohi   Radiant

8

Aniani	Cool, refreshing; to blow softly as a breeze; also a mirror
Ano	Peacefulness, sacredness, feeling of awe, oppressive quiet, lost in thought
'Ano'i	Lover, beloved, desired one
'Ano'i pua	Cherished flower, sweetheart
'Ano-lani	Chief-like nature, of heavenly or royal character; celestial, noble, royal, pure
Ānuenue	Rainbow
Anuhea	Cool, soft fragrance as of upland forests; sweetness, a mountain breeze
Ao-lani	Heavenly cloud
Ao-loa	Long cloud; high or distant cloud; Fig., a distinguished person
Aouli	Blue vault of heaven; firmament, sky
Ao-wena	Rosy cloud
'Āpua-kea	A beautiful maiden changed by Hi'iaka into the rain that bears her name; a name associated with Ko'olau-Poko, O'ahu
Auali'i	Royal, chiefly
'Aukai	Seafarer
Au-kanai'i	A strong warrior; Lit., a strong current
'Au-kele-nui-a-Iku	A hero in a favorite Hawaiian legend who overcame his jealous brothers and was given supernatural powers. He went to the underworld for the water of life; later he visited the sun, moon, and stars. Lit., great travelling swimmer, son of Iku. Can be shortened to 'Au-kele

9

'Auli'i	Dainty, neat, perfect
Aumoe	Midnight, Lit., time to sleep
'Awapuhi	The flowering ginger, the root was used to scent and dye tapa
Ea	Sovereignty, rule, independence; life, breath
'Ea'ea	Spray, sea spray; dignified, honorable
'E'ea	Quick, ready, expert
'E'e'e	To keep climbing over everything, as an active child; mischievous
'E'ehia	Overcome with fearful reverence; awe-inspiring, solemn; fear, reverence, awe
E'ehu	Healthy, also Ehuehu
'E'e-kuahiwi	Climber of mountains
'E'elekoa	Stormy
'E'ena	Shy, timid, wary, wild, untamed; extraordinary
'E'epa	Extraordinary, incomprehensible, peculiar, as persons with miraculous power. Many 'e'epa characters in legends were born in unusual forms— a plant or animal
'Eha-koni	Throbbing love, Lit., throbbing ache
Ehehene	Laughter, to laugh merrily, to giggle in glee
'Ēheu	Wing, as of a bird
'Ehu	Spray, foam, mist Dusty Reddish tinge in the hair of some Polynesians
Ehuehu	Animation varying from fury and storm to power and

	majesty; violent, furious, powerful, anger, admiration, majesty
	Healthy
'Ehu-kai	Sea spray, foam; the name of a wind at Hālawa
'Ele'ele	Black, dark; the black color of Hawaiian eyes
'Ele-hiwa	Coal-black, jet-black, all black
'Ele'ī	Blue-black, shiny black. Fig., select, choice
'Ele'io	To go after secretly and speedily; agile, spry; the name of a famous runner on Maui
'Elemoe	Dark, still, as sea or forest; sea-green, jet-black, sacred black
'Elepaio	Native Hawaiian forest bird. This bird was believed to be the goddess of canoe makers.
'Eleu	Active, alert, nimble, lively
'Elewawā	Dark and tumultuous, as sea or forest
'Ena	Red-hot, glowing
	Shy
	Abundance
'Ena-aloha	Intense affection or longing
'Ena-makani	Strong wind
'Eno	Wild, untamed, fearful of people; also 'Eno'eno, very wild
'Eu	Mischievous, naughty, as a child
'Eu'eu	Exciting, rousing, alert, lively, animated
Ēwe	Sprout, lineage kin, birthplace, family trait
Ēwe-kapu	Sacred or kapu lineage
Ēwe-lani	Chiefs of divine descent

Ha'aheo	Proud, haughty
Haku	Lord, overseer, master. A chief was often addressed as E ku'u haku – my master.
Haku·mele	To weave a song, hence a poet.
Hālana mālie	Calm tranquillity
Hale·lehua	A sea goddess who lived in the depths of the channel between O'ahu and Kaua'i, Lit., Lehua blossom house.
Hale·mano	Hero of a romantic tale who woos a beautiful but fickle Puna princess, Lit., many houses
Hali'a	Sudden remembrance, especially of a loved one
Hali'a·aloha	Cherished or loving memory
Hāli'i·maile	Spreading maile vine
Hā·loa	Son of Wākea, the first man, by his own daughter. Taro is a symbol of Hā·loa and descent from Hā·loa is a sign of ancient heritage. Lit., long life
Halolani	To move quietly, as a soaring bird
Halulu	Roar of water or wind, thunder; also a legendary man-eating bird
Halulu·ko'ako'a	A god with a wind form living in the low-spreading rainbow. He made the winds roar, Lit., coral roaring
Hana·aloha	Love sorcery
Hānai·a·ka·malama	A benevolent goddess, Lit., foster child of the moon
Hana·kahi	An ancient Hilo chief, Lit., single task
Hanini	To pour down, as heavy rain

Hanohano	Glorious, honored, dignified, distinguished
Hau kea	Snow, snow white
Hau-lani	A daughter of Hina, Lit., royal ruler
Ha'u-lili	Kaua'i god of speech, Lit., trilling chatter
Haumakapu'u	God who watched over fish ponds, Lit., lord with bulging eyes
Haumea	The earth-mother goddess, great source of female fertility, she presided over childbirth, Lit., red ruler (red was considered a sacred color)
Hau-nani	Handsome or splendid ruler
Hau'oli	Joy, happiness, also Hau'oli'oli
Hā'upu	Recollection
Haupūehuehu	Snowflake
Hekili	Thunder, Fig., passion, rage
Hemolele	Perfect, faultless, holy, pure in heart; angel
He-pua-laha'ole	A flower not common; one who is as choice and highly prized as a very rare blossom
Hiapa'i'ole	Foremost, expert
Hiapo	First-born child
Hie	Attractive, distinguished, noble, becoming; can also be Hiehie with the added meaning superb
Hi'iaka-i-ka-poli-o-Pele	Pele's favorite sister, she figures in many legends and was worshipped by hula dancers, Lit., Hi'iaka in the bosom of Pele
Hi'iaka-i-ka-pua-'ena'ena	Sister of Pele who in one form was a healer and guide to travellers lost in the

13

	wilderness, Lit., Hi'iaka in the smoking heat
Hi'ialo	A beloved child borne in the arms; a child who stays close to a parent
Hi'i-lani	Held in the arms of heaven
Hi'ilawe	To lift or carry; name of the highest waterfall in Hawaii at Waipi'o Valley
Hi'ilei	To carry, tend, and cherish a beloved child
Hikia-lani	Facing or looking up to heaven; the name of a beautiful O'ahu princess
Hina	Probably the most widely known goddess of Polynesia. She was the goddess of the moon and is involved in many legends and has many specialized forms.
Hina-'ea	Goddess of sunrise and sunset. A healer, especially of 'ea'ea, a childhood disease; and an expert tapa maker
Hina-i-ke-ahi	Mother of the demigod Maui, Lit., Hina in the fire
Hina-kula-i-ua	Goddess of the rain
Hina-lau-lima-kala	Possibly the most beautiful of all the Hina goddesses. She lived on the bottom of the sea and was the goddess of kahunas skilled in medicines from the sea, Lit., Hina leaves of limu-kala
Hīnano	The male pandanus flower
Hina-'ōpū-hala-ko'a	Goddess of corals and spiny creatures of the sea, Lit., Hina stomach-passing coral
Hina-puku-'ai	Goddess of food plants; in the form of an 'elepaio she would

14

	guide canoe-makers to appropriate trees, Lit., Hina gathering plant food
Hina-puku-i'a	Goddess of fishermen; Lit., Hina gathering seafood
Hinuhinu	Bright, glossy, lustrous; glittering, as of polished stones or shells; splendid, splendor
Hiwahiwa	Precious, beloved, esteemed; a favorite
Hiwa lani	Esteemed chief; beloved child or favorite
Hoaka	Crescent, as on a helmet or of the new moon; splendid, bright, to flash as lightening; Fig., glory
Hoa-koa	Soldier-friend
Hoa kua	Godly companion; companion of a god
Hoa pili	Close companion. The name given by Ka-mehameha to his closest friend
Hōkeo	A god who assisted Lono in bringing the winds to Hawai'i
Hōkū	Star
Hōkū-'ai-'āina	Navigator star, Lit., star ruling land
Hōkū ala	Rising star
Hōkū-ao	Morning star; the planet Venus when seen in the morning
Hōkū-helele'i	Falling stars
Hōkū-ho'okele-wa'a	Sirius. The appearance of this star was the signal of sailing on a voyage; Lit., canoe guiding star
Hōkū-lani	Star in the sky
Hōkū-le'a	A navigator star, probably Arcturus; a zenith star above

15

	Hawai'i; Lit., clear or happy star
Hōkū-lele	Shooting star
Hōkū-li'ili'i	Small star
Hōkū-noho-aupuni	A name for the Milky Way; Lit., ruling star
Hōkū-pa'a	Immovable star, the North Star
Holokai	Seafarer
Holo'oka'a	Paramount, supreme
Hone	Sweet and soft as music; sweetly appealing as perfume or a memory of love; mischievous. Also Honehone
Honi	To kiss, a kiss; formerly to touch noses on the sides in greeting
Ho'ohie	To make beautiful, elegant, delightful, also Ho'ohiehie
Ho'okele	Navigator, helmsman
Ho'ola'i	To enjoy peace; to poise aloft as a bird; calm, peaceful
Ho'olaua'e	To cherish, as a beloved memory
Ho'opa'a	To make fast, to bind
Hōpoe-lehua	Tall lehua tree in full bloom. In a Pele legend Hōpoe is a maiden changed into a balancing rock at the ocean's edge at Puna. The lapping of the waves against the rock suggests the movements of the hula, so Hōpoe is considered famous as a hula dancer
Huaka	Clear as crystal, bright, dazzling
Hua-lani	Offspring of a chief
Huali	Bright, polished, clear, pure white, gleaming morally pure

16

Hua-nanai   Name of the hinahina root when used in love sorcery, Lit., swift fruit

Hua-pala   The orange trumpet flower; sweetheart in the sense of 'sweetie-pie'; like the expression 'a peach' for a handsome boy or pretty girl, Lit., ripe fruit

Hu'e-lani   Opening up to heaven

Hū'eu   Witty, amusing; mischievous, rascal

Hulu-ali'i   Royal favorite and loved one; Lit., royal feather

Huna-kai   Sea foam; also the white flowered beach morning glory and the sanderling, a small shore bird that migrates to Hawai'i in the winter

'Iao   The name of Jupiter appearing as the morning star, Fig., dawn

Ihe   Spear

'Ihi-lani   Heavenly splendor; sacredness of a chief

Ihupani   Expert, wise person. Lit., closed nose, perhaps referring to deep diving and hence profound knowledge

Ikaika   Strong, powerful

'Ili-ahi   All kinds of the Hawaiian sandalwood

Ilihia   Stricken with awe, reverence; thrilled, as by beauty

'Ilima   The flower of O'ahu, related to hibiscus, the small yellow-orange blossoms are strung into handsome leis

'Imi ā loa'a   Discoverer, to seek until found

'Imi-hau   Name of a stormy wind at Lahaina. Lit., dew seeker

'Imi-'ike   Seeker of knowledge

'Imi-loa   To seek far, distant traveller; Fig., one with great knowledge

'Imi-pono   To seek or strive for righteousness

'Imina   Seeking

Inoa   Namesake

Inoa-'ala   Esteemed name, especially of a chief; Lit., fragrant name

'Iolana   To soar, poise, as a hawk; soaring hawk

'Io lani   Royal hawk, symbol of royalty because of its high flight in the heavens

'I'o pono'ī   One's own flesh and blood

'Io-uli   Dark hawk, also a bird god

Ipo   Sweetheart, lover

'Iu   Lofty, sacred, revered, consecrated, e.g. Ka-'iu-lani – royal, sacred one

'Iu'iu   Majestic, lofty; a distant realm of the gods

'Iwa-lani   Heavenly 'iwa bird. The 'iwa, frigate or man of war bird. Fig., 'iwa = thief because frigate birds steal food from other birds; also used Fig., for a handsome person

Ka-'ahu-manu   The favorite wife of King Kamehameha I, later kuhina nui. The name means bird feather cloak

Ka-'ahu-pāhau   Chiefess of the shark gods of Pearl Harbor who protected

	O'ahu from sharks. Lit., the well-cared for garment
Ka'alokuloku	Intrepid, fearless, as of one unafraid to brave the elements
Ka'aona	The name of a month; attractive when referring to a child. Children born in the month of Ka'aona were thought to be attractive and lovable (June 7-July 6)
Ka'apeha	Cloud of several colors reaching over the heavens, frequently a sign of rain; impressively big, even fat in a distinguished manner; influential and important
Ka-'au-moana	Seafarer
Ka-'elele-o-ka-wana'ao	The messenger of the dawn
Kā'eo	Full, as a food calabash. Fig., full of knowledge; strong, zealous. Also Kā'eo'eo
Ka-ha'i	A legendary hero who travelled to Samoa and brought back breadfruit to O'ahu.
Kaha-ka-'io-i-ka-mālie	The 'io (hawk) poises in calm. Said in admiration of a handsome person).
Kahakea	High, inaccessible, as a cliff
Ka-haku-loa	The tall lord
Ka-hala-o-māpuana	The youngest of four sisters who appear in many Hawaiian legends. Lit., the pandanus wafted fragrance
Ka-hala-o-puna	A beautiful Mānoa princess. Her husband suspected her of unfaithfulness and killed her three times, each time she was rescued by the owl god,

19

	Pue'o-ali'i, Lit., The hala of Puna.
Ka·hanu	The breath
Ka·hau·lani	The dew from heaven
Ka·hau·o·lupea	The dew which weighs down the flowers
Ka·hekili	The thunder
Kahe·wai	Water flowing
Kahiau	To give generously or lavishly with the heart and not with expectation of reward
Ka·hiki·lani	The arrival of the chief
Ka·hikina	The arrival, the east
Kāhiko-o-ke·akua	Adornment of diety, a poetic name for rain
Kāhili	Feather standard symbolic of royalty; segment of a rainbow (a rainbow was considered a sign of royalty)
Ka·honi	The kiss. In ancient Hawai'i to 'kiss' was to touch noses in greeting.
Ka·hūnā	The hidden one
Kai	Sea
Kai·aka	Shadowed sea
Kai·apo	Rising or high tide; Lit., encircling sea
Kai·ea	Rising tide, sea washing higher on land than usual; Lit., rising sea
Kai·emi	Ebbing sea; Lit., decreasing sea
Kai·halulu	The roaring sea
Ka·'ihi·kapu	The kapu sacredness
Kai·hohonu	Deep sea, high tide
Kai·ho'i	Ebbing sea; Lit., returning sea
Kai·holo	Running sea or current
Ka'ī·i·mamao	The far distant supreme (one)

Kai·kāne	Strong sea; Lit., male sea
Kai·kea	Sea foam, white sea
Kai·kō	Sea with a strong current
Kai·malolo	Quiet sea, as in a calm cove
Ka·'imi	The seeker
Ka·'imi·lani	One seeking heaven
Kai·moku	Turning of the tide, Lit., cut sea
Kai·nalu	Sea wave
Kai·nehe	Whispering sea
Kai·nui	High tide, big sea
Kai·nu'u	High sea
Kaiona	Goddess who lived in the Wai'anae Mountains and was said to have pet birds who could guide anyone lost in the forest back to his companions.
Kai·palaoa	In legends a boy who was an expert in riddling and punning, Lit., whale sea
Ka·ipo	The sweetheart
Kai·po'i	Breaking waves or surf
Ka·'iu·lani	The highest point of heaven; royal sacred one. The name of Hawai'i's last and possibly most beautiful and tragic princess.
Kai·ulu	Sea at full tide; mounting sea
Kai·'ūpoho	Breaking sea, breakers, white caps; Lit., resounding sea
Kakahi	Solitary, unique, outstanding
Kakahiaka·nui	Early morning
Kaka'ikahi	Rare, precious
Kākuhihewa	One of O'ahu's most famous chiefs who appears in many legends.
Ka·lā	The sun, sunshine
Ka·lā·heo	The proud day

Ka·lā·kaua	The day of battle; name of the last king of Hawai'i
Ka·lā·hiki·ola	The life bringing sun
Ka·lama	The torch
Ka·lani	The chiefly one
Ka·lani·ana·'ole	The royal chief without measure
Ka·lani·kāula	The royal prophet
Ka·lau·o·ka·lani	The multitude of the royal chief
Ka·leho	The cowry shell
Ka·lei	The wreath of flowers; the beloved
Ka·lei·kau·maka	The beloved child to be looked upon with pride and love
Ka·lei·kini	The many leis
Ka·leo·aloha	The voice of love
Ka·leo·nahenahe	The soft and gentle voice
Kamaehu	Strength, energy, firmness of resolution
Kamaha'o	Wonderful, astonishing, remarkable
Kamahele	A far reaching, strong or heavy branch; the main branch
Kama hele	Traveller
Kamahoi	Splendid, marvelous, wonderful
Ka·maile	The fragrant maile vine
Ka·makana	The gift
Ka·maka·nui·'aha'ilono	A god who introduced the art of healing, Lit., the great eye messenger
Ka·mālamalama·o·nā·lani	The light from the heavens
Kama·lei	Beloved child
Ka·māmalu	The protection
Ka·malu·o·nā·lani	The peace of the heavens

22

Ka-mana-kai	The sea power
Kamani	A large seashore tree whose hard wood was used to make calabashes
Ka-mea-ho'okoho-'ia	The chosen one
Ka-mea-'i'o-makamae	The truly precious one
Ka-mehana-o-ka-lā	The warmth of the sun
Ka-moho-ali'i	The companion of kings. Name of the legendary shark god, king of the ocean and Pele's older and favorite brother
Ka-mole	The main root, the foundation
Ka-mo'o-ali'i	The chiefly mo'o
Ka-mu'o-o-ka-lani	The young leaf bud of heaven; a chief's child.
Kana	A Maui demi-god who could take the form of a rope and stretch from Moloka'i to Hawai'i
Ka-na'ina	The conquering
Ka-na'i-aupuni	Conqueror of the nation
Ka-nani	The beauty
Kāne-hekili	God of thunder
Kāne-hoa-lani	A god who ruled over the heavens, a father or ancestor of Pele, Lit., royal companion of Kāne
Kani-lehua	Mist-like rain famous at Hilo; Lit., rain that the lehua flowers drink.
Ka-noa	The free one
Ka-noe-lani	Heavenly mist
Ka-nuha	The sulky one
Ka-nupa	The luxuriant growth
Ka-'ohi-nani	Gatherer of beautiful things, gathering beauty
Ka-'ohu	The mist

Ka-'ohu-lei-lani	Bedecked with heavenly leis
Ka-'ōnohi-o-ka-lā	The center of the sun
Ka-pa'a	The firm, steadfast
Ka-pahu	The drum
Ka-pahu-kapu	The kapu (sacred) drum
Ka-paka	The raindrops, the patter of the rain
Ka-palai-'ala	The fragrant fern
Kāpi'i	Curly; a person with curly hair. Persons with curly hair were believed to be strong hence good warriors.
Ka-pili	One of Princess Likelike's names, Lit., the relationship or the pili (grass)
Ka-pi'o-lani	Sacred arch of heaven
Ka-pi'o-lehua	The lehua arch
Ka-pono	The righteous
Kapolakā	Mysterious, unfathomable
Kapo-'ula-kīna'u	Goddess with a dual nature - a benevolent hula goddess identified with Laka and as a fierce goddess of sorcery; she was a sister of Pele and daughter of Haumea. She was more frequently known as Kapo.
Ka-pua	The blossom
Kapua'i-akua	Footprint of a god; Fig., the foot of the rainbow
Ka-pua-'ilima	The 'ilima flower
Ka-pua-i-milia	The beloved flower or child
Kapu-āiwa	Mysterious kapu, a name of Ka-mehameha V
Ka-pū'ali	The warrior (see pū'ali)
Ka-pueo	The owl
Kapukapu	Dignity, regal appearance; entitled to respect and reverence

24

Kapukawai	To be handsome and noble
Ka-pule	The prayer
Kapu-likoliko	The opening royal bud, name of a daughter of Ka-meha-meha I
Ka-puna-kea	The clear spring or the white coral
Ka-puni	The favorite one
Ka-pū-o-alaka'i	A forest goddess who presided over the lines (pū) by which new canoes were guided (alaka'i) from the mountains to the sea
Ka-ua-noe	The misty rain
Ka-ua-'oliko-ka-lani	The rain sparkling in the sky
Ka-uhi	A demigod who was chained to a cliff at Kahana Bay by Pele, he was turned into a rock formation today called Crouching Lion. His full name was Ka-uhi-'īmaka-o-ka-lani, the observant cover of the heavens
Ka-u'i	The beauty
Kau-i-ke-aouli	The sign placed in the blue sky; the familiar name of Ka-mehameha III
Kau-i-ke-o-lani	Placed on heaven's peak (Kau-i-ke-(a)o-lani)
Kauila, Kauwila	A native tree whose hard wood was used for spears and mallets
Ka'uka'ulele	Nimble, active, joyful, as one leaping for joy
Ka'uka'u lua 'ole	Dauntless, quick, alert
Kaulana	Famous, celebrated; resting place, restful, quiet
Kaula uila	A streak of lightening
Ka-'ula-wena	The rosy glow of dawn

Kaulele	Soaring on the wing; extraordinary
Kauluwela	Glowing, bright-colored,colorful
Kau-mahina	Moon rise
Kau-mai-ka-'ohu	The mist rests
Kauna'oa	The plant emblem of the island of Lana'i; The slender orange stems are woven into leis
Kauoha	Order, command, will; to order or command
Kaupili	Mutual love, beloved friend
Ka-wa'a-o-Maui	The canoe of Maui
Ka-wa'a-loa	The long canoe
Ka-wai-māpuna	The bubbling water
Ka-wēkiu	The highest point
Ka-wēkiu-lani	The royal height (a name of Princess Ka-'iu-lani)
Ka-welo	A legendary hero born on Kaua'i, the name means the family trait
Ka-wena	The rosy reflection in the sky
Ke-ahi	The fire
Ke-ahi-lele	The firebrand; the name of a star
Ke-aka-o-ka-lani	The shadow of heaven
Ke-ala	The pathway
Ke-'ala	The fragrant
Ke-ala-hou	The new pathway
Ke-ala-ke-kua	The pathway of the god (Ke-ala-ke-(a)kua)
Ke'ale	The wave, the crest of the wave
Ke-'ale-wai-hau-a-ke-kua	The snow water wave of the gods (it was believed that the gods made snow).
Ke-aloha	The loved one, beloved

26

Ke-aloha-pau'ole	Love never ending
Ke-'alohi	The brightness; also the name of a star
Ke-'alohi-lani	The shining heaven, the brightness of heaven
Ke-ao-melemele	The daughter of Kū and Hina who excelled in chanting, hula, and surfing
Ke-au-hou	The new era
Keawe	Name of a southern star, said to be named for an ancient chief; one whose lineage goes back to antiquity
Keha	Height, pride, dignity, lofty, majestic, also Kehakeha; additional meaning is to brag or boast
Kēhau	Dew, mist, dewdrop; name of a gentle land breeze
Kēhau-lani	The dew of heaven
Kei	One's pride and glory
Ke-kai-loa	The distant ocean
Ke-kai-malu	The peaceful sea
Ke-kau-lani	Placed in the heavens
Ke-kau-like	The equality; sister of Queen Ka-pi'o-lani, mother of Kuhio and Ka-wānana-koa
Keiki-lani	Child of heaven
Ke-kipi	The rebel
Ke-koa	The soldier, the courageous one
Ke-kua-ao-ka-lani	The spirit of heaven; leader of the adherents to the old religion who rebelled against the actions of Ka-mehameha II
Kela	Excelling, reaching high above
Kēlau	To put out first leaves

27

Keli'i	The chief
Keli'i-maika'i	The good chief, the name of Ka-mehameha's younger brother
Ke-liko-a'ela-ka-ua-i-ke-kai	Rain sparkling on the sea
Ke-'ohi	The harvest
Ke'oke'o	White, clear
Ke-ola	The life, patron star of Lana'i
Ke'o-lani	Heaven's continuation, name of a demi-goddess of healing
Ke-'ōpu-o-lani	Gathering clouds of heaven. Name of a wife of Ka-mehameha, mother of Ka-mehameha II & III, (Ke-'ōpu(a)-o-lani)
Keoua, Keaoua	The rain clouds. The name of several famous chiefs of the 18th century, among them the father of Ka-mehameha
Kia'i-makani	Watcher of the wind
Kiakahi	Person of fixed purpose; alone, unique, only one
Kiha-nui-lūlū-moku	The fierce lizard guardian of Pali-uli, a mythical paradise on Hawai'i; Lit., great island-shaking lizard
Kiha-wahine	A Maui chiefess who at death became a goddess worshipped on Maui and Hawai'i; Lit., female lizard
Kīkaha	To soar, poise, glide
Kilakila	Majestic, strong, tall, imposing; having poise that commands admiration
Kilo	Stargazer, reader of omens
Kilohana	Best, superior, excellent; the highest point. Lit., the name of the outside, decorated sheet of tapa (the best one)

Kilokilo	Enchantment, magic
Kilo lani	Predictor who can read signs in clouds
Kio·pa'a	North Star; Lit., fixed projection
Koa	Brave, bold, fearless; soldier, warrior, hero; The largest of the native Hawaiian forest trees formerly used for making canoes, surfboards, and calabashes.
Koa·lau·nui	A kind of koa tree regarded by the Hawaiians as male, Lit., large-leafed koa
Koa·li'i	Chiefly warrior
Koapaka	Valiant, brave, especially in war.
Kohā·i·ka·lani	Resounding in the sky
Ko'i'ula	Rainbow-hued rain, mist, cloud
Koke	Quick, swift runner
Kōkua	Helper, comforter
Kōlea	Pacific golden plover. A migratory bird which comes to Hawai'i about the end of August and leaves early in May for Siberia & Alaska. Fig., one who becomes prosperous and leaves with the wealth.
Kolonahe	Gentle, pleasant breeze; gentle, mild
Kolopua	Fragrant, as air laden with the perfume of flowers
Konakona	Strong, bulging with muscles
Kōnane	Bright moonlight, to shine as the moon; bright, clear; an ancient game resembling checkers
Konapiliahi	Strong, powerful
Kōnea	Restored to health

Kōnunu	Rounded, well-shaped, as a lehua flower
Kuaehu	Silent, still, lonely
Kūākāhili	One of high birth who stands by a kāhili - the feather standard beside the chief
Kua-kini	Innumerable, brother of Ka-'ahu-manu and a governor of the Big Island who enforced puritanical laws
Kū-ali'i	One of the last great Hawaiian chiefs, it is said he died in 1730 at the age of 175!
Kua-nalu	Surf just before it breaks; place where the surf breaks
Kūha'o	Standing alone, independent Fig. unusual, extraordinary as rain from a clear sky
Ku'iaumoe	Privileged and trusted; persons in a chief's retinue
Kū kamaehu	To stand firmly
Kūkilakila	Majestic, regal
Kūkini	Runner, swift messenger
Kū-lani	Suitable to heaven
Kūlia	To strive; outstanding, fortunate
Kūlia-i-ka-u'i	Outstanding beauty
Kū-moku-hāli'i	A god of forests and canoe makers, Lit., Kū-island spreader
Kumu	Base, foundation; beginning, source
Kumu-kahi	A figure in Hawaiian legends, the name means first source
Kumu-mau	Eternal source
Kumu-nalu	The source of waves; where surfing starts
Kū'oko'a	Independent, free
Kūo'o	Serious and dignified

Kūpaʻa	Steadfast, firm, immovable, loyal
Kūpaoa	Strong permeating fragrance, as of jasmine
Kūpapalani	Chief of the highest rank; state of heavenly foundation
Kūpono	Upright, honest
Kupuʻeu	Rascal, scamp Hero, wonderous one, so called because the hero of legends, often as a youth, was fond of plundering taro and stealing chickens.
Kupulau	The spring season, Lit., leaf sprouting
Kū uaki, Kū uwaki	Sentinel, guard
Kuʻu aloha	My love
Kuʻu-ipo	My sweetheart
Kū-ʻula-kai	The god of fisherman, built the first fishpond; the name means red (or sacred) Kū of the seas.
Kuʻu-lei	My beloved; Lei (a wreath of flowers) can also mean a beloved child, wife, husband, sweetheart
Kuʻu-lei-lani	My heavenly lei
Kuʻu-maka	An affectionate term used by the grandmother of Kamapuaʻa, the pig god, rather like 'apple of my eye'
Kuʻu-momi-makamae	My precious pearl, a beloved person
Laʻa-hana	Patron goddess of tapa makers, Lit., work dedicated
Laʻa-kea	Sacred light, as sunshine, happiness, knowledge
Laʻa-maomao	A goddess of the winds, Lit., distant sacredness

31

La'a'ula	Autumn, Lit., red time (of leaves)
La'a ulu	Spring, time of growth
La'ela'e	Bright, serene; calm, pleasant
Lae o'o	An expert, Lit., mature brow
Lae 'ula	Well-trained, clever person Lit., red-brow, red being a sacred color
Lā hiki	Eastern sun, rising sun
La'i	Calm, stillness, quiet as of the sea, sky, wind; peace, contentment, silence
La'ikū	Great calm, quiet, peace, serenity
Laka	Gentle, tame; to treat with kindness; Goddess of the hula, the maile and other forest plants; also a legendary hero and canoe god.
Lako	Rich, prosperous
Lālama	Daring, fearless, clever, as a climber of precipices or trees
Lālauahi	Gray, stormy-looking, smoke colored
Lālea	Buoy, beacon, prominent landmark ashore to steer by
Lama	Torch, light, lamp. The wood of the lama, a kind of ebony, was used for torches to light hula altars and because of this the word suggests enlightenment.
Lamakū-o-ka-na'auao	Torch of wisdom, said of great thinkers
Lamalama	Fair-complexioned; bright looking, animated, vivacious; another meaning of this word is torch-fishing
Lamalama ka'ili	To glow with health

Lana	Buoyant, floating; to lie calm at anchor, calm, still as water.
Lanaau	To float or drift with the current; wander, ramble, drift aimlessly
Lanakila	Victory, triumph
Lani	The sky, heavens, heavenly; a very high chief, royal, high-born, aristocratic, also Lanila-ni; The use of this name is of great antiquity and designates high honor.
Lani-ali'i	Heavenly chief; the name for the yellow allamanda
Lani-kua-ka'a	Poetic name for a very high chief; the highest heaven
Laniloa	Vast sky, tall majesty
Lani nu'u	Highest heavens, an epithet for royalty
Lā-ola	Day of life
Laua'e	A fragrant fern this also means beloved, sweet, of a lover
Laule'a	Peace, happiness, friendship; restoration of a disrupted friendship
Lawa	Enough, sufficient, ample; possessed of enough or ample knowledge, hence, wise, capable; also strong
Lawakua	Strong-backed, muscular, of strong physique, bulging with muscles. Fig., to be a dear friend or companion
Lea	Goddess of canoe makers, who with her sister goddess, Hina-puku-'ai, would take the form of an 'elepaio bird and help canoe makers choose appropriate trees for canoes

Lehia	Skilled expert
Lehiwa	Admirable, attractive
Lehua	The flower of the 'ōhi'a tree, also the flower of the Island of Hawai'i. Fig., a warrior, a beloved friend or relative, a sweetheart, an expert
Lehua-nani	Beautiful lehua blossom
Lei	A wreath or garland of flowers, shells, feathers. Fig., a beloved child, wife, husband, sweetheart or younger sibling
Lei-'ā'ī	Lei for the neck. Fig., A beloved person, especially a mate or child
Lei-ali'i	Royal lei, chief's lei; crown, diadem
Lei-aloha	Wreath of love, Fig., a beloved child
Lei-hulu	Feather lei, formerly worn by royalty, Fig., dearly beloved child or choice person
Lei-lani	Heavenly lei, royal child
Lei-Lono	Lono's lei
Lei-nani	Beautiful lei
Lelehua	Skillful; a good thinker
Lele-ua	Wind-blown rain
Le'o	Lofty, tall
Leo-ho'onani	A song of praise, hymn
Leo-lani	Heavenly voice
Le'o-lani	Lofty, tall; chiefly height, rank
Leo-mana	Voice of authority
Lewa-lani	Highest stratum of heaven
Līhau	Gentle, cool rain that was considered lucky for fishermen; cool, fresh as dew-laden air
Li'i	The smallest; often the youngest child in a family is affec-

34

	tionately called this. Also a shortened form of ali'i—chief
Liko	Leaf bud, newly opened leaf. Fig., child, especially the child of a chief.
	Shining, glistening with dew, sparkling
Lile	Bright, shining, dazzling, sparkling
Lili'i	Tiny, dainty, fine
Lilinoe	A goddess of the mists and younger sister of Poli-'ahu, goddess of the snow, Lit., mists
Lino	Bright, shining with splendor, brilliant; calm, unruffled. Also Linolino
Linohau	Dressed to perfection, beautifully decorated
Loa	Long, far; very much, very good
Loea	Skillful, expert, clever, applies especially to women
Lohe-lani	Hear heaven's bidding
Lōkahi	Unity
Loke	Rose (an English form)
Loke-lani	Heavenly rose
Lokomaika'i	Gracious, generous, benevolent
Lolopua	Zenith, the highest point
Lono-maka-ihe	A god of spear throwers, Lit., spear point Lono
Luala'i	Same as Luana
Luala'i-lua	Two-fold tranquility
Luana	Content, to be at leisure, to enjoy pleasant surroundings
Lua'ole	Superior, incomparable, unequaled, second to none
Luhiehu	Beautiful, attractive, festooned

Lulu	Calm, peace, protection; to lie still, as a ship in harbor; to be calm, as the sea
Lunalilo	Away up high
Māhea	Hazy, as moonlight
Māhealani	Night of the full mon
Mahi'ai	Farmer
Māhie	Delightful, charming, pleasant; also Māhiehie
Mahina	Moon, moonlight
Māhinahina	Pale moonlight
Māhoa	To travel together in company, as canoes
Māhuahua	Thrive, flourish, grow strong
Maiele	Eloquent, skilled in speaking
Maika'i	Good; good-looking, handsome; beautiful, good health
Maikohā	Deified hairy man who became the god of tapa makers. From his grave grew the first wauke plant
Mā'ila	Light brown, as the skin of some Hawaiians Clear, as the ocean on a sunny day when the depths can be seen
Maile	A native twining shrub with shiny fragrant leaves used for leis and decoration. Laka, goddess of the hula, was invoked as goddess of the maile; in legends four sweet-scented sisters.
Ma'i-ola	A god of healing, Lit., cured sickness
Mai-poina-ia'u	Forget-me-not
Maka	Beloved one, favorite one; maka also means eye, face, sight

36

Maka-'ālohilohi	Eyes bright and sparkling; blue or light brown eyes
Mākaha	Fierce, savage, ferocious. Name of a star said to be a patron of fighters
Makahehi	Admiration, desire for, wonder, amazement; attractive; to admire
Maka-hihiu	A person of exceptional merit or lineage
Maka-hī'ō	Eyes that dart in every direction, as if looking for mischief; a mischievously alluring look
Maka-hou	Beginning, new start
Maka'ike	To see clearly and with keen powers of observation; to see more than most, esp. to see supernatural things; to have the gift of second sight
Maka-'imo'imo	Twinkling eyes; also the name of a constellation in the Milky Way
Maka-'io-lani	Eye of the royal hawk, the name of a star
Makakai	Sea-washed; spray
Makakēhau	Heart's desire, Lit., dew eye
Maka-koa	Bold, fierce, unafraid
Makalapua	Handsome, beautiful; to blossom forth
Maka-launa	Friendly, having many friends, sociable
Maka-le'a	Twinkle-eyed, happy-eyed; mischievous
Maka-lehua	Lehua flower petals, Fig., attractive (as young girls), lovely as lehua flowers
Makali'i	Tiny; also the name of a chief of Wai-mea, Kaua'i. Because of his fame as an agriculturist

	his name was given to a month and the summer season; the Pleiades also were called by his name and by some he was considered a navigator
Makamae	Precious, of great value, highly prized, darling
Makamaka	Intimate friend
Makamaka hānai	Generous and hospitable friend
Makamaka-nui	One with a host of friends because of a genial, kindly, or hospitable nature
Maka mua	First child of a family, Lit., first end
Makana	Gift, present, reward, prize
Makana-aloha	Gift of friendship or love
Makanahele	Wild, untamed; of the wilderness or forest
Maka-nani	Beautiful eyes
Makani	Wind
Makani-ke-oe	A wind god who could make plants grow and could take the form of a tree, Lit., wind of the trailing whistle
Makanoe	Mist-laden; a variety of lehua tree that grows on Mt. Wai'ale'ale on Kaua'i
Makoa	Fearless, courageous, aggressive
Māla'e	Clear, calm, serene, as a cloudless sky
Mālama	To take care of, caretaker; fidelity, loyalty
Mālamalama	Light of knowledge; shining, clear
Mālana	Buoyant, light; to move along together; also the name of a star

38

Mālie	Calm, quiet, still
Malina	Calming, soothing
Malino	Calm, quiet, as the sea; peaceful, as one's spirits
Mali'o	Dawn light; twilight, especially as it pierces the shadows of the night; also a mythical woman renowned for entertaining with music and with her ability in love magic
Mali'u	Well-salted; Fig., seasoned with wisdom
Malu	Shade, shelter, protection, peace; the stillness and awe of taboo
Maluhia	Peace, quiet, serenity, safety; the solemn awe and stillness that reigned during some of the ancient taboo ceremonies
Malu-lani	Under heaven's protection
Mamao	Far, distant, high in rank
Mamo	The black Hawaiian honey creeper, its yellow feathers were used in the finest featherwork
Mamo ali'i	Descendant of a chief
Mana	Spiritual or divine power
Mana loa	Great power, almighty
Mana'o-akamai	Spirit of wisdom
Mana'o'i'o	Faith, confidence
Mana'olana	Hope, confidence, to hope; Lit., floating thought
Mana'opa'a	Determined, resolute
Mana-piha	Absolute power, supreme
Manō	Shark, Fig., passionate lover
Mano-ka-lani-pō	An ancient Kaua'i chief, Lit., many gods of heaven
Manomano	Great in number; magnificent; powerful

Manono	The presistent one, name of a famous chiefess who died fighting beside her husband
Manu	Bird
Manu-wai	Water bird
Māpu	A rising fragrance, wind-blown fragrance wafted, bubbling, splashing as water.
Māpuana	Sending forth fragrance
Māpu mai ke aloha	Love pours sweetly forth
Māpuna	Bubbling spring, Fig., surge of emotion Also Māpunapuna
Mau	Always, steady, constant, unceasing
Maua'ālina	Powerful, strong, of superior strength, athletic
Mauli	Life, heart, seat of life
Mauliauhonua	Descendant of old chiefs of a land
Mauli hiwa	Choice or precious life
Mauli ola	Name of a god of health, breath of life, power of healing
Mau-loa	Everlasting
Mauna	Mountain
Mauna-kū-wale	Mountain standing alone
Mau-'oli'oli	Ever joyous
Mea 'a'a	Adventurer
Mea 'ē	Extraordinary, unusual, strange, wonderful
Mea-ho'omana'o	Souvenir, keepsake
Mea-kālia	The waited for one
Mea-kia'i	Guard, preserver, protection
Mea-la'a	Consecrated or holy one
Mea-laha-'ole	Something rare, choice
Mea lanakila	Champion, winner
Mea makamae	Precious object, treasure

Mea-mana'o-nui-'ia	Person constantly in mind
Mea-nui	Beloved person or thing (sometimes said sarcastically)
Mea'ono	Cake of any kind, pastry, cookie; lit. delicious thing
Mea'ono-'ōhelo-papa	Strawberry shortcake
Mea wiwo'ole	Intrepid person, adventurer
Me'e	Hero, heroine; important person, admired, prominent
Mehameha	Loneliness, solitary, hushed silence-as during the hush of taboo
Mele	Song, chant of any kind, poem; to sing
Mele-ho'āla	Song to wake a sleeping child, especially one composed for a chief's child or a favorite child; Lit., awakening song
Mele ho'ālohaloha	Serenade
Mele ho'oipoipo	Love song
Melemele	Yellow; also the name of a star
Melia	Plumeria
Mikihilina	Most beautiful, said of dress, finery, ornaments
Mīkololohua	Eloquent, fascinating in speech; delightful, entertaining. Also Mīkolelehua
Miliani	Gentle caress
Mililani	To praise, to give thanks; to treat as a favorite
Milimili	Toy, plaything; favorite, beloved; darling
Mili-nanea	Cherished person that absorbs and delights, also Milimili nanea

Mimo	Gentle, of upright character, quiet, capable; deft but un-assuming
Minamina	Regret, be sorry; sorrow To prize greatly, esp. something in danger of being lost; also miserly
Mino'aka	Smiling, to smile
Moana	Ocean, open sea
Moani	Light or gentle breeze, usually associated with fragrance; windblown fragrance
Moani-'ala	Fragrant breeze
Moani-lehua	Wind-borne fragrance of lehua blossoms; said to be the name of a wind at Puna
Moano-nui-ka-lehua	A goddess who came with Pele from Kahiki, she had two forms—one of a woman as beautiful as a blossom-laden 'ōhi'a lehua and another as a moano (goatfish)
Moemoeā	Dream of a cherished wish (whether good or bad)
Mōhā	Fully developed, as a flower; of fine physique, as a person
Mohala	Unfolded, as flower petals; blooming, as a youth just past adolescence; shining forth, as light
Mō'ī	King, queen, sovereign, ruler
Mō'ike	Dream interpreter
Mokihana	A native tree found only on Kaua'i and the flower of that Island. The fragrant berries are strung into leis
Mololani	Well cared for; place on O'ahu where the god Kāne drew the figures of the first man

42

Momi	Pearl; Ni'ihau name for a shell used in leis
Mo'o-i-nanea	The mother of all the mo'o (lizard) gods and goddesses
Mōpua	Melodious, pleasant, of a voice
Na'au-ali'i	Kind, thoughtful, forgiving, possessed of aloha, Lit., chiefly heart
Na'auao	Learned, intelligent
Nā-'ēheu-o-ka-pō	The wings of the night
Nae'ole	Never weary
Nahenahe	Soft, sweet, as music of a gentle voice; gentle-mannered, soft-spoken
Nā-hiku	Constellation of the Big Dipper, Lit., the seven
Nahoa	Bold, defiant, daring; also Nehoa
Nākolo	Roaring, as of surf or thunder
Nā-lani	The heavens
Nale	Clear, bright; also Nalenale
Nalu	Wave, surf; full of waves
Nānā-honua	Gazing earthward; the angel's trumpet tree
Nānā-i-ka-lani	Gazing heavenward
Nanea	Fascinating, enjoyable, tranquil, relaxed
Nani	Beauty, glory, splendor; beautiful, splendid; beautiful flower; also Naninani
Nani ahiahi	Everlasting beauty, also a flower name, the four-o'clock
Nani ali'i	Name for the yellow allamanda, Lit., chiefly beauty
Nani-kōkī	Supremely beautiful (name of Umi's ivory pendant)
Nani-loa	Most beautiful

Nani makamae	Precious, exquisite
Nani mau loa	Everlasting beauty, also a flower name, the everlasting or straw-flower
Nani Wai'ale'ale	A native violet found only in high bogs on O'ahu and Kaua'i. Lit., Wai'ale'ale beauty
Nā-one	The sands
Nā-pua	The blossoms, the flowers
Naupaka	Native shrub found in the mountains and near the coast; its half-flowers recall a legend of parted lovers
Nēnē hiwa	Prized, beloved, precious
Niau	Moving smoothly, swiftly, silently; flowing or sailing thus
Ni'o	Highest point, pinnacle; to reach the summit
Niolo	Stately, tall and straight as a tree without branches; also sleepy
Niolopua	Handsome; also the god of sleep
Niuhi	Man-eating shark. This name was used in sayings to mean a powerful warrior because it was believed that a chief or warrior who could capture this shark would acquire something of its nature
Niu-loa-hik[i]	God of coconut trees who had three forms - an eel, a man, and a coconut tree
Noe	Mist, rain, spray, misty; to settle gently, as a mist
No'eau	Clever, skillful, wise, artistic
Noe-lani	Mist of heaven
No'eno'e	Quiet, sedate; also a printed tapa

Noe-'ula	Pink mist, as that about a rainbow
Nohea	Handsome, lovely, of fine appearance
Nohe'o	Mischievous, rascal
Nohi	Bright-colored, vivid, as the rainbow
Noho loa	North Star
Nono	Rosy-cheeked; sun burned
Nonohe	Attractive, beautiful
Nonohina	White blossoms of the olopua tree
Nui	Large, big; great, important
'Oehu	Prancing, leaping; blustery, gusty, as a storm or angry person
Ōhāhā	Flourishing, plump, healthy
'Ōhelohelo	Pink, rosy, the color of 'ōhelo berries
Ohi	Young animal; a maiden just entering womanhood
'Ōhi'a lehua	The tree of the Island of Hawai'i, famous in song and legend; see Lehua
Oho lupalupa	Abundant, luxuriant (as plants or hair tresses)
'Ōhua palemo	Young of the uhu (parrot fish); Fig., a clever person who gets away with mischief, Lit., slippery young
'Ol'ol	A superior person; sharp, pointed
Ola	Life, health; recovered, healed
Ola-ka-inoa	The name lives on, said of a child bearing the name of an ancestor
Ola-loa	Long life
'Oli	Joy, happiness

'Oliko	Shiny, sparkling, bright, also 'Oliliko
'Olili	Shiny, sparkling, shimmering, as moonlight
'Olina	To make merry, joyous
'Ōlino	Bright, brilliant, dazzling
Olo-lani	Acclaimed, as a chief
Olopua	Lovelorn, heart-broken; also a large native tree with hard, dark wood used for spears and digging sticks
'Olu	Comfortable, gentle; cool, refreshing; kind, courteous; also 'Olu'olu
'Ōmea	Beloved, respected person; reddish, murky
Onaona	Soft, sweet fragrance; gentle and sweet
'Onipa'a	Immovable, steadfast (this was the motto of Ka-mehameha V and Lili'u-o-ka-lani)
'Ono	Delicious, also 'Ono'ono
'Ōpua-lani	Heavenly rain clouds
'Oumuamua	Name of foremost soldier in battle or in the front rank of battle
'Ouo, 'Ouwo	Young animal or person, youthful, sprightly
Pa'a-lima	Held in the hand
Pa'aloha	Keepsake, memento
Pai'ea	An edible crab, one of the names of Ka-mehameha the Great, Fig., star athlete
Pa'ihi	Clear, bright; tidy, well-dressed in one's best, honored
Pā-i-ka-lani	Reach the sky
Pa'iniu	Native Hawaiian lilies with long, narrow, silvery leaves

46

Pā-ka-lā	The sun shines
Pākela	A great person who excells
Pākela nani	Glory that excelleth
Pākeu	To surpass
Pākeupali	Excessively great, greatly exceeding
Pala luhiehu	Golden yellow, a beautiful yellow as of the kauna'oa vine
Palanehe	Noiseless, quietly, dainty; to move in a dainty fashion
Pali-loa	Distant or tall cliff, Fig., distant, aloof aristocratic
Panepo'o	Pinnacle, summit; most important
Pano	Dark, as clouds; obscure, deep blue black; Fig., unapproachable as the unknown, (said of very high chiefs believed to be of divine descent). Also Panopano
Pano pa'u	Glossy, glistening black
Papa lani	The upper heavens, heaven and all the spiritual powers
Pau-mau-no'ono'o	Keepsake, memento, Lit., all continuing thoughts
Pawa	The darkness just before dawn
Pele	The fire and volcano goddess. The Hawaiians resented the giving of this name unless it was revealed in a dream.
Pi'i-kea	Daughter of Pi'i-lani, married to Umi, the name means the life ascends
Pi'i-lani	To climb to heaven; the name of a famous Maui chief
Pīkake	The Arabian jasmine with its fragrant white flowers. Since

47

	Princess Ka-'iu-lani was fond of both these flowers and her peacocks (pīkake) the same name was given to both.
Pilialo	Bosom friend, beloved wife
Pili-aloha	Beloved companion, close friend
Pili-'au-ko'i	A trusted friend
Pilikua	A giant; beloved husband
Pili-lani	Close to heaven
Pohihihi	Mysterious, bewildering
Pohokano	Able counselor
Pohu	Calm, quiet as the sea after a storm
Po'i	Top or crest of a breaking wave. Also Po'ina
Po'ikū	Over-powering, as love
Po'ina-kai	Cresting of the sea
Po'iu	Afar, very high; glorious, sacred
Pōki'i	Younger brother or sister, often spoken affectionately
Pōlani	Handsome, beautiful; clean, pure
Pōlehulehu	Twilight, dusk
Poli'ahu	Name of the beautiful goddess of snow who was said to live on Mauna Kea
Polikua	The dark invisible beyond, as beyond the horizon
Polinahe	Soft and gentle, as love, music or a breeze; Slim-waisted and broad shouldered
Polohiwa	Dark, glistening black
Pololei	Straight, upright, correct
Pōmaika'i	Good fortune, prosperity; lucky
Ponia	Consecrated

48

Pono	Goodness, excellence, moral, upright, successful, in perfect order
Pono'ī	One's own
Ponopono	Neat, tidy; wealthy
Po'okela	Foremost, best, superior, champion
Pua	Flower, blossom
Pua ahi	Name of a star; Lit., fire flower
Pua-'ala	Fragrant flower
Pua ali'i	Descendant of a chief
Pua aloalo	Hibiscus blossom. The hibiscus is the state flower of Hawai'i
Pua'ehu	To shine brightly, as red flowers
Pua'ena	To glow brightly
Pua-hau	The hau blossom; name of the grand-daughter of Ka-meha-meha
Puahi	To glow like fire
Puahia	Spry, quick
Puakea	Pale-colored, especially a tint between white and pink, as sunset clouds
Pua-laha-'ole	A choice and rare flower; Fig., a beloved person, Lit., flower not spread
Pualalea	Clear and bright
Pua-lanalana	Floating flower
Pua-lani	Descendant of a chief, Lit., heavenly flower
Pua-lei	Flower lei; cherished blossom or child
Pua-lē'ī	Flower that attracts many
Pū'ali	Warrior, so called because Hawaiian fighters tied (pū'ali) their malos at the waist so no flap would dangle for a foe to sieze.

Pua-nānā-lā	Sunflower. Lit., flower looking (at the) sun
Pua-nani	Beautiful flower
Pueo-kahi	An owl god of Hana. Lit., single owl
Pūhau	Cool spring
Puīa	Fragrant
Puka-lani	Heaven's door
Pukana aloha	Souvenir of a beloved, gift from a loved one
Pulelehua	Butterfly; blown in the air, as spray
Pūloku	Comely; bright, sparkling as sun or dew
Pumehana	Warm-hearted, affectionate
Punahele	A favorite or precious child, Lit., a spring that goes on
Punia	A son of Hina famous in legends for tricking sharks, he was swallowed whole by the chief of the sharks and lived for ten days in the belly of the shark
Pūnihi	Lofty, majestic, dignified
Pūnohu	Rainbow lying close to the earth
Pūnono	Gorgeously red, filled with sunshine, ever beautiful
Pūnua	Young bird or fledgling, Fig., young child or sweetheart
Pu'ō-lani	Gathered heavenward
Pu'ukalahala	Redeemer, one who helps in time of trouble
Pu'ukani	Sweet voiced
Pu'uwai hāmama	Generous, open-hearted
Pu'uwai-hao-kila	Heart of steel, courageous
Ua	Rain. Rain was beloved as it preserved the land. It was

	called, kahiko o ke akua, adornment of deity
Uakea	Mist, mist-white; white as breaking surf or snow
Ua-kini-maka-lehua	Name of a mountain rain Lit., rain of countless lehua blossom faces
Uakoko	A low-lying rainbow, reflection of rainbow colors in the clouds, Lit., blood rain
Ua-ma-ka-lau-koa	Name of a rain at Nu'u-anu, Lit., rain amid the koa tree leaves
Ua-moaniani-lehua	Name of rain at Puna, Lit., rain that wafts the fragrance of lehua blossoms
'Uao or 'Uwao	Conciliator, peacemaker
U'i	Youthful, handsome, beautiful, heroic
Uila, Uwila	Lightening, also electricity
U'i-lani	Heavenly beauty
U'i launa 'ole	Beautiful beyond compare
Ukali ali'i	The planet Mercury, so called because it follows so close to the sun. Lit., following the chief
'Ula	Red, scarlet; brown as the skin of Hawaiians
	Sacred, regal (probably because red was a sacred color)
	Blood
'Ūlili	The sandpiper or wandering tattler bird, a winter migrant to Hawai'i
Ulu-aloha	Inspired with love
Ulu-koa	Name of a star, Lit., soldier's inspiration
Ulu-lani	Inspired of heaven; heavenly grove

Ulumaheihei	A very close friend of King Ka-mehameha I; He was the king's most trusted friend and it was to him that King Ka-mehameha entrusted his bones after his death. King Ka-mehameha renamed him Hoapili
Uluwehi	Growing in beauty; a place where beautiful plants thrive
Waha-mana	Voice of authority, Lit., powerful mouth
Wai	Water, liquid of any kind other than sea water; wai has a connotation of wealth and life
Waiakua	Distant, aloof, as a chief too high to mingle with others, Lit., godly blood
Wai-'ala	Perfume, cologne, Lit., fragrant water
Wai-'ale'ale	Rippling water
Wai-'apo	Water caught in a taro leaf, often used in ceremonies as it was regarded as pure in not having touched the ground, Lit., caught water; Fig., a beloved mate
Wai-lana	Calm, quiet, as the sea, still water; Banished for unworthy conduct A prayer uttered to free a kapu period
Wai-lani	Rain water, especially that used in medicine and purification, Lit., heavenly water
Waileia	Name of a morning star
Wai-lele	Waterfall, Lit., leaping water

Wai-nani	Beautiful water
Wai-'oli	Singing water
Wai'olu	Cool, pleasant, attractive, soft, gentle, pleasing
Wai-pua	Honey of flowers
Wai-puhia	Wind-blown water, especially the spray of a waterfall
Wai-puna	Spring water, Fig., a sweetheart
Wana'ao	Dawn
Wānana	Prophecy
Wehi	Ornament, decoration; a song honoring someone
Wehi-lani	Heavenly adornment
Wehiwa	Choice, prized, a choice object
Wēkiu	Topmost, summit; of the highest rank
Wena	Glow, as of sunrise or fire; a close relationship, a blood relative
Wena'ula	Red glow
Wiwo'ole	Fearless, brave, bold
Woa	Calm
Wohi	A high chief exempt from the prostration kapu

4

Creating a Hawaiian name

Creating a Hawaiian name requires knowledge of the Hawaiian language. You cannot just pick a word that "sounds nice." A friend told me that she had decided to name her first baby girl ILINA because it sounds so pretty. Fortunately, she had three boys and no little girl was given a lovely sounding Hawaiian name which means cemetery!

So, the first rule to follow in selecting or creating a Hawaiian name is:

1. BE CAREFUL

Even a simple word or name should be checked by someone who knows the Hawaiian language.

Here are a few additional suggestions:

2. The same Hawaiian word will frequently function as a noun, verb, adjective, and adverb. Thus, ALOHA can mean love, loved one, to love, and loving.

3. In Hawaiian the adjective follows the noun. For example PUALANI is heavenly (LANI) flower (PUA).

#4. The definite article—the word THE—is KE or KA in the singular (KA PUA—the flower) and NĀ in the plural NĀ PUA (the flowers). KE is used before all words beginning with K and, in general KA precedes everything else. However, KE is used before certain words beginning with A, E, O, P, and ' —this will usually be noted in the Hawaiian-English dictionary.

5. Observe carefully the placement of the macrons (—) and glottal stops ('). These markings can totally change the meaning of a word. For example: moi = threadfish; mo'i = to remain long in one place; and mō'ī = king, queen, majesty.

6. If you wish to use the Hawaiian equivalent of an English word, be sure to cross-check your choice in the

Hawaiian section of the dictionary. For example, you might decide that you would like to use the Hawaiian word for 'joy' as a name. If you look in the English to Hawaiian section of the dictionary you will be given several Hawaiian words meaning joy—HAU'OLI, 'OLI, 'OLI'OLI, LE'A, LE'ALE'A. For whatever reason your first choice might be LE'A. If you now cross-check this word in the Hawaiian section of the diction- ary you will find that LE'A does indeed mean joy, but it is also strongly associated with the joy of sex with meanings of sexual gratification and orgasm also!

Finally, do not let all of these rules and cautions make you afraid of the Hawaiian language. There are many beautiful and poetic words in the Hawaiian language— the names of winds, stars, clouds, legendary heroes and beautiful princesses. Perhaps looking for a Hawaiian name will be, for you, the beginning of a love and appreciation of the Hawaiian language.

5

About Names and Naming In General

Since ancient times, people have believed there is magic surrounding a person's name. In many primitive societies it was believed that a person's name was sacred and could not be revealed without giving away a part of one's self.

Although we do not feel quite so strongly about names today, there is still a great deal of truth in the saying—"You are your name." In fact, as a parent, one of the most important things you can give your child is an appropriate name. This section will give you some guidelines on name selection, but first, let's look briefly at the psychology of names.

Your name is frequently the first (and sometimes the only) impression you will make on another person. It may be unfair, but it is true, that your name can pre-dispose people to think of you as a winner or loser, as attractive or unattractive. Why else would so many celebrities change their names? Would you wear Ralph Lipshitz (now Ralph Lauren) jeans? Would Marion Michael Morrison (movie star John Wayne) ever have become the stereotype for the macho cowboy?

Many adults have learned to cope with, or at least to accept with equanimity, a peculiar or inappropriate name. But for children, an unusual or unattractive name can be very traumatic. Studies have proven that children who consider a surname derisive will transfer their feelings about the name to the person who bears it. The same is true of given names. If Linda and Robert are perceived as attractive and energetic and Olga and Hubert as dull and unattractive, Linda and Robert will begin to see themselves as attractive and energetic and Olga and Hubert will see themselves as dull and unattractive.

Other people are the mirror in which we see ourselves. We begin to establish our self image based on the reaction of other people toward us. If our name elicits a negative reaction, we begin to see ourselves in a negative manner—and eventually, begin to behave in accordance with that image. If Bertha is treated as homely and unfashionable, she may indeed become so!

In 1976, Dr. Thomas V. Busse, an educational psychologist, did a study of children's attitudes toward first names. In the study 2,500 children, ages 9 to 13, were asked what names they preferred and what names they disliked. Boys preferred names like John, David, Michael, Robert, Mark; girls liked names like Linda, Carol, Barbara, Susan, Diane, Lynne. Unusual names like Stockton, Carlton, Phoebe, and Lola May were scorned.

Recalling her childhood, a woman named Electra writes, "That name was a blight, a plague—it was like lugging around an extra leg, or having another eye sprouting out of the middle of my forehead. You know how terrifically cutting kids can be, and naturally, they are going to grab on to something like that."*

The conclusion of Dr. Busse's study was: "If parents want their children to be bright, popular and successful, they should give them popular names. It's cruel for parents to give kids odd names."

Long before our era of psychological studies a well-known author wrote, "Some names stimulate and encourage the owner, others deject and paralyze him."

Choosing a child's name is indeed an important responsibility for any parent. The following guidelines may provide some help in making a good selection.

1. Don't be humorous, cute, or fanciful when matching a given name and a surname. Candy Barr, Christian Church, Ima Hogg—may make you smile, but could make the child given these names cry!

2. Be careful of names that are ultra-unusual, hard to pronounce, or spelled in an unusual manner. It isn't any favor to 'Alice' to spell her name 'Alys'—no one else will spell it that way and when the time comes for her to sign legal documents it could prove more than just inconvenient.

Weschler, Lawrence. "Profiles", The New Yorker, 11-17-86, p. 54.

On the other hand, don't pick a name that is too common. Remember the cartoon where the teacher calls on Jason and 50% of the boys in the classroom stand up! There are fashions in names just as there are fashions in clothing. There are well over 10,000 names in current use, but about 85 percent of all newborns will receive names from the top 100 on the list of today's most popular names.

The short lists below show the top five boys' and girls' names on birth certificates in Hawaii and illustrate how these names have changed since the early 1900's.*

Boys' names	1909-1914	1950	1981
1.	John	John	Christopher
2.	William	Michael	Michael
3.	George	Robert	David
4	Antonio	William	Jason
5.	Joseph	Dennis	Justin
Girls' names			
1.	Maria	Linda	Jennifer
2.	Mary	Kathleen	Jessica
3.	Amelia	Sharon	Nicole
4.	Helen	Carol	Crystal
5.	Elizabeth	Charlene	Melissa

3. Think carefully about names that are uni-sex. Some older names like Joyce and Marion just aren't used for boys anymore. Other uni-sex names like Lee or Robyn seem fine for either sex but most boys would prefer an unequivocally masculine name.

4. Pay attention to the initials that are created when you combine given, middle, and surname. For example Peter Ian Grant and Felicia Ann Tongg sound just fine but the initials P.I.G. and F.A.T. are not.

5. Listen to the sound of the total name. Say the full name aloud. A full name generally sounds best when the number of syllables of both names combined is uneven. Surnames of one syllable usually combine best with given names of two or four syllables. For example, last names like Tam or Kent follow more smoothly behind first names like Martin or Melinda rather than Mark or May. With surnames of two syllables like Hudson or Goto, try using given names of one or three syllables like Ann, Melissa, Mark or Christopher.

---

*Ronck, Ron. Ronck's Hawaiian Almanac, p. 114.

When the surname has three syllables, a given name of two syllables usually sounds best.

Many of the most common Island surnames of Japanese origin are four syllables—Nakamura, Okamoto... With these names a one or three syllable given name is most pleasant sounding.

With surnames of more than four syllables brevity is best when choosing a given name—not only is a long name inconvenient, but it will probably be abbreviated. Poor Elizabeth Yanagihara—by the time she has written her name the rest of the class will be on the second test question!

6. Be aware of any associations a particular name has acquired. For example both Gay and Dick have sexual meanings in popular slang.

Names can also rise and fall in popularity in association with celebrities, movies, etc. In 20 years no one may remember the movie *Rambo* but your child could be stuck with this unusual name for a lifetime.

7. Once you have selected a name, try it out. Say it aloud several times. Run it by friends, teachers, business associates, and see how they react to it. Ask for their comments and suggestions. Trial and error is one way to come up with a winner.

8. Finally, if you also believe there is magic in names, check the origin and meaning of the name you have chosen. Perhaps a child whose name means gracious or courageous will be just that.

There are also some legal requirements about names and naming in Hawai'i. A birth certificate must be filed with the State Department of Health within seven days after the birth of a baby. The birth certificate will usually be made out for you at the hospital. However, it is your responsibility to check the spelling of the baby's first, middle, and last name and the spelling of all other names that appear on the birth certificate.

If you cannot decide on a name at the time of birth, the birth certificate can be filed with only the baby's last name. Within 90 days, however, you must report the baby's given name or names to the State Department of Health.

Remember, changing a name can be expensive. Even a change in spelling is a legal procedure, and may require a legal change of name decree.

I hope this brief guide will help you to choose a pleasing and suitable name for your new son or daughter. If you would like to know more about the fascinating history and psychology of names you will find a reading list at the end of this book.

6

Your English Name, Its Meaning and a Hawaiian Equivalent

HE AHA KŌ LOKO O KOʻU INOA?
WHATʼS IN MY NAME?

This section consists of an alphabetical listing of many of the most often used English names along with their origin and meaning. If you find your name in this listing, you will not only discover its meaning in English, but will also learn a suggested Hawaiian word or words that correspond in concept to the original meaning of your name.

Using this section you can find a Hawaiian name that is an authentic part of the Hawaiian language and not simply a string of letters from the Hawaiian alphabet.

Until now, there were only three ways to acquire a Hawaiian name: 1. It could be given to you at birth; 2. it could be given to you as gift, a sign of affection and respect, by someone of Hawaiian ancestry; or, 3. you could 'transliterate' your non- Hawaiian name into Hawaiian.

This book presents a fourth method, but first it is necessary to explain transliteration and its problems. Transliteration is the process of replacing the letters of one language with the letters of another language. One needs to look at a bit of Hawaiian history to understand how and why English words were transliterated into Hawaiian in the first place.

In 1778 Captain James Cook became Hawaiʻi's first tourist. Capt. Cook's voyages to Hawaiʻi and his published journals set the stage for a large scale invasion of the Hawaiian Islands by Europeans and Americans.

By 1820 missionaries from the English-speaking world were arriving in Hawaiʻi with the express purpose of converting the natives to Christianity. The Hawaiian language never had a written form. These early Christian missionaries were eager to put the Hawaiian language in writing so that schools could be opened and the Bible and prayers could be translated into Hawaiian.

Twelve letters of the English alphabet were chosen—A, E, H, I, K, L, M, N, O, P, U, W—to represent the sounds of the Hawaiian language. Using these twelve letters it was possible to begin to record the Hawaiian language and to publish books, newspapers, whatever, in Hawaiian.

Native Hawaiians who converted to Christianity were given a Christian name at baptism. Since most native Hawaiians did not speak English, it was necessary to 'Hawaiianize' the Christian name- creating what we call a Hawaiianized-English name. This Hawaiianized-English name was created by the process of transliteration. That is, the letters in the English name that did not occur in the Hawaiian alphabet, were replaced by one of the twelve letters of the Hawaiian alphabet.

The formula for transliterating is as follows:

The English letters		this Hawaiian letter
B,F,P		P
C,D,G,J,K,Q,S,T,X,Z		K
H	are	H
N	replaced	N
L,R	by	L
V,W		W
Y		I

Therefore, if you want to Hawaiianize the English name BARBARA, you must replace the B's and R's with letters of the Hawaiian alphabet. Looking at the above formula B becomes P and R becomes L, so we have PALAPALA for BARBARA (the extra A is added because, in Hawaiian, consonants are always separated by a vowel).

Many words were, and continue to be, added to the Hawaiian language by this method. Unfortunately, with names, the Hawaiianized-English name thus created frequently does not sound like a Hawaiian word, or has a very unappealing, unmelodic sound. Most often a transliterated name has no meaning whatsoever. However, in some cases, a transliterated name coincides with a real Hawaiian word. Sometimes this Hawaiian word will have a neutral or even complimentary meaning. But, occasionally, the Hawaiian word will have a negative or undesirable meaning. For example, the Hawaiianized-English version of Frank is PALANI, which is a native Hawaiian word which has as one meaning stinky!

In this book another method of Hawaiianizing your English name is proposed. The original meaning of your English name is translated (not transliterated) into a suggested Hawaiian word or phrase that is equivalent in concept.

Let's take a closer look at the names listed in this section using ALAN as an example. First the English name and its variations (ALAN, ALLEN) are given; then masculine or feminine forms (LANA, ALANA). Forms from other languages, diminutive or pet forms, and variant spellings are also noted here.

Next is the origin of the name followed by its meaning or meanings: "ALAN is from the Gāelic and means handsome."

Remember, most of our names come from quite ancient sources, so, at times, both the origin and meaning of certain names can be lost in history. I have tried to be as accurate as possible. A list of the sources consulted is in the back of this book.

Next, in capital letters, is the suggested Hawaiian word (or words) thought to best express the meaning of this name. Continuing with our example of ALAN, the Hawaiian word would be NOHEA, meaning handsome and of fine appearance.

Our suggested equivalent will frequently not be the only possible equivalent. We have chosen the equivalent we consider the most appropriate or appealing. Once you know the meaning of your English name you might want to continue to explore the Hawaiian language for additional equivalents.

Finally, if the Hawaiianized-English form that has commonly been used (the transliteration) corresponds exactly to a native Hawaiian word or to another Hawaiianized-English word, the meaning of that word will be noted. For example, the Hawaiianized-English form of ALAN, ALLEN, and ALANA would be ALANA which is the native Hawaiian word for awakening.

If the Hawaiianized-English form does not coincide with a native Hawaiian word or another Hawaiianized-English word, no note is made of this form.

There are some English names that have no Hawaiian equivalent. If your name happens to be one of these, you might want to use your middle name or even surname's meaning to find an equivalent Hawaiian name.

The names we have included were chosen from a listing of the most popular names in current usage.* Since there are many thousands of given names we could not include every name. If your name has been omitted, please let us know. Perhaps it can be included in future editions.

Hawaiian equivalents to the English names listed have been selected exclusively from the Hawaiian-English Dictionary (1957), and the Hawaiian-English, English-Hawaiian Dictionary (1971, 1986), all by Mary Pukui and Samuel Elbert.

As Pukui warns in the introduction to the 1971 dictionary, "literal translations from one language to another are impossible." Also, in Hawaiian, as in every other language, there are words or phrases that may have acquired sexual, vulgar or obscene connotations. The primary meanings of all suggested Hawaiian equivalent names have been carefully checked. In so far as possible, suggested Hawaiian names with 'other meanings' have been avoided or so noted.

---

* *Dunkling, Leslie Alan. The Guinness Book of Names, pp. 32-40.*

AARON is from the Hebrew and means high or lofty mountain. The Hawaiian for this name could be MAUNA 'IU (lofty mountain) or perhaps MAUNA KEA (literally white mountain) would be appropriate. MAUNA KEA on the island of Hawai'i is the highest mountain in the world if measured from its base under the Pacific Ocean to its top—almost 32,000 feet compared to Mt. Everest's 29,028 feet.

ABIGAIL and its variations ABBEY, ABBIE and GAIL are from the Arabic and the Hebrew. The meaning is a father's joy or a source of joy. KUMU 'OLI is the Hawaiian, KUMU (source) and 'OLI (joy, happiness, pleasure).

ABRAHAM and the variations ABRAM, ABE, and BRAM are from the Hebrew and mean exalted father; father of multitudes. The Biblical Abraham was the founder of the Hebrew nation. In Hawaiian KĀMEHA'IKANA means a multitude of descendants, KĀMEHA'I (wondrous) and KANA (many). The goddess Haumea was sometimes called by this name because she is said to have had numerous children by one husband, then to have returned later as a young woman and again had numerous more children; she did this for many generations producing 'a multitude of descendants.'

ADA is a short name with several possible origins and meanings. From the Latin it could mean noble birth; from the German—happy; and a Biblical meaning is beauty or ornament. Several Hawaiian meanings from each of its origins could be: PUA-LANI, descendant of royalty; HAU'OLI, happy; and LINOHAU, beautifully decorated or ornamented.

The Hawaiianized-English form of ADA is AKA, a native Hawaiian word meaning shadow.

ADAM is Hebrew for man of red earth. In the Biblical story of creation, God created the first man from the soil of Palestine which is red, therefore, the first man was called ADAM. In Hawai'i a KAMA'ĀINA is a person born in Hawai'i or a long time island resident, its literal meaning is 'child of the land.' Another variation could be KĀNE O KE 'ALAEA. KĀNE means man and 'ALAEA is a type of red soil that was

---

Hawaiianized-English forms of names are given only if they correspond exactly to a native Hawaiian word or another Hawaiianized-English word.

used in medicine and a purification ceremony.

ADELAIDE with its variations ADELE, ADELLA, ADELINE, and the German ELSA /ILSA all originate in an ancient German word that was used as a royal title thus these names all mean noble. LANI ALI'I in Hawaiian would mean heavenly chief, royal chief, or noble chief.

ADOLPH is from the Old High German and means noble wolf. It was used among the German tribes for persons of the nobility. Since there are no wolves in Hawai'i the closest equivalent would 'ĪLIO LANI or simply LANI: 'ĪLIO (dog) and LANI (noble). The ancient Polynesians brought dogs with them on their original voyages to Hawai'i. The dogs were sometimes household pets, but were more often raised to be cooked in the imu and eaten.

ADRIAN, and the feminine forms ADRIENNE and ADRIANA are from the Greek meaning rich and the Latin meaning black or dark one. The name referred originally to residents of the ancient town of Adria, which gave its name to the Adriatic Sea, and was famous for its black sand. KAIMŪ is the spectacular black sand beach of the Puna district of Hawai'i, so this seems like an apt Hawaiian equivalent for this name; another possibility would be HIWA which means a sacred and desirable black.

AGATHA is from the Greek and means good and kind. St. Agatha, the patron saint of Sicily, is the protectress against volcanoes and earthquakes. MAIKA'I in Hawaiian means good, beautiful and kind.

AGNES, the Italian form INES, the Spanish form INEZ, and a Manx form NESSIE all stem from the Latin and Greek and mean purity and chastity. In the Christian religion there are six St. Agneses all known for their innocence and chastity. MA'EMA'E is the Hawaiian word for clean, pure, attractive and chaste.

AILEEN see EILEEN

ALAN, ALLEN, the feminine forms LANA, ALANA, and LANE which can be both masculine and feminine have several different origins. From the Gāelic the meaning is handsome; from the Celtic the meaning is harmony and peace; and from the Norman, cheerful. The first reported bearer of this name was Alawn, a legendary British poet of the first century. NOHEA meaning handsome and of fine appearance could be the masculine for this name, with MALUHIA meaning peace and serenity the feminine form.

The Hawaiianized-English of ALAN, ALLEN, and ALANA would be ALANA, the native Hawaiian word for awakening; LANA and LANE would be LANA meaning buoyant.

ALBERT and the feminine forms ALBERTA and ALBERTINE are from the German and mean noble and bright. 'ALOHI LANI means the brightness of heaven. The individual parts of this Hawaiian word perfectly express the meaning of this name. 'ALOHI (bright, brilliant), and LANI (heaven and also a very high and noble chief).

ALEXANDER is an ancient name and has many variations: ALEX, ALEC, the Scottish; ALISTAIR, the Gāelic; and the Russian SASCHA are the masculine. Feminine forms are ALEXANDRA, ALEXA, ALEXIS, SANDRA,and SONDRA. The Russian is SACHA. The diminutive SANDY can be both masculine and feminine. The origin of this name is Greek and it means defender or protector of men. The name is most closely associated with Alexander the Great who in ancient times conquered the known world.

In Hawaiian KA MEA KIA'I I NĀ KĀNAKA means a preserver and protector of men; a simpler form would be MEA KIA'I, protector.

The Hawaiianized-English form of SANDRA would be KANELA meaning a canal, a Hawaiianized-English word; of SANDY it would be KANI, a native Hawaiian word meaning sound (as in music).

ALFRED, and the feminine forms ALFREDA and ELVA are from the Anglo-Saxon and mean elf counsel or wise helper. In ancient times elves were held to be wee, supernatural beings of great wisdom who provided mortals with good advice. In ancient Hawai'i the elfin folk are known as MENEHUNE. The menehune, or little people, performed good deeds for mortals, but only at night when they could not be seen. The Hawaiian word for an able counselor was POHOKANO.

ALICE, and the variations ALIX, ALLISON, ALYSON, ALICIA, and ALISSA are from the Greek and mean truthful; or from the German via French meaning noble. In Hawaiian LANI is noble and KŪPONO is honest and truthful.

ALISTAIR, see ALEXANDER

ALMA is from the Latin and means kind and loving. In the Hawaiian language ALOHA is a special word embodying love, kindness, and much more.

ALVA, ALBA, are both from the Italian and mean white or fair. In Hawaiian KEA is white and used to refer to a person of fair complexion. In the royal courts of old Hawai'i fair-complexioned persons were often favorites.

ALVAN, ALVIN, ALWIN, ALWYN, and the feminine ALVINA are from the Teutonic and mean noble friend and loved by all. The Hawaiian HOALOHA, or HOA ALOHA means beloved friend and combines the words for friend (HOA) and the word for love (ALOHA).

ALYSIOUS, see LEWIS

AMANDA and the more popular shortened form MANDY are from the Latin and mean lovable. In Hawaiian HENOHENO means lovable and sweet.

AMBER is an Arabic word meaning jewel. Brownish-yellow beads made from amber (a fossil resin) were used in ancient times to ward off disease. The closest Hawaiian equivalent would be MEA MAKAMAE meaning a precious object, a treasure.

AMY and AIMÉE are from the Latin via French and mean the beloved. MEA ALOHA is the Hawaiian for loved one.

ANDREW, ANDERS, ANDY, DREW and the feminine forms ANDREA and ANDRINA are all from the Greek word for man. This name has come to mean manly and courageous. St. Andrew is the patron saint of Scotland. KOA is a Hawaiian word for brave and valiant, and is a name that could be used for both boys and girls. The KOA tree is the largest of the native Hawaiian forest trees. Its beautiful wood was used in ancient times for canoes and surfboards, and in modern times it is used for fine furniture.

ANGELA, ANGELICA, ANGELINA, ANGIE are from the Greek and Latin; the Greek means a messenger and the Latin an angel or heavenly being. Angels were the messengers of God. In ancient Hawai'i the messenger of a chief was 'AULANI. This combines two Hawaiian words: 'AU (to travel by sea) and LANI (heavenly).

ANN. This popular name has over 100 variations throughout the world. Some of them are: ANNA, ANNE, ANNETTE; the Slavonic diminutive ANIKA; the Spanish diminutive ANITA; and NAN, NANCY, NANETTE. ANN is the Greek and Latin form of the Hebrew HANNAH meaning grace. In Christian legend St. Ann was the mother of the Virgin Mary. The Sanskrit ANNAPURNA was the goddess of plenty. A Hawaiian form for this name could be MAIKA'I. In addition to grace, MAIKA'I means excellent, beautiful, righteousness, and well-being. The Christian prayer "Hail Mary, full of grace"...begins in Hawaiian "Aloha 'oe e Malia, ua piha 'oe i ka MAIKA'I . . ."

The Hawaiianized-English form of ANN and ANNA is ANA which is a native Hawaiian meaning to measure or a cave; NAN = NANA which means to weave and is also the name of a star and a variety of taro.

ANNABEL, ANNABELLA is a combination of Ann and the Latin belle-beautiful so the name means Anna the beautiful. For ANN we have used MAIKA'I meaning grace and beauty. For this name we could add LOA making MAIKA'I LOA, meaning very beautiful, much beauty.

ANTHONY the feminine forms ANTIONETTE, ANTIONIA and the shortened form TONY used for both boys and girls are from the Latin name Antonius. This was the name of a Roman clan and is claimed to mean greatly esteemed and praiseworthy. For the masculine the Hawaiian could be HIWA LANI which means esteemed chief; and for the feminine PUA ALOALO or PUALOALO, which is the word for the hibiscus flower. ALOALO also means loved and served by many.

APRIL is from the Latin, to open up. Originally it referred to the opening up of the earth at the spring season. The name AVERILL, a possible masculine variation is April's child. With Hawai'i's year round tropical climate there was no word in the ancient Hawaiian language for the spring season. However, the word KUPULAU means leaf sprouting, a sure sign of spring in the cold climates where this name originated.

ARDITH. See EDITH.

ARETHA is Greek for the best. In Hawaiian the best is KA 'OI. The island of Maui has as its motto—Maui no ka 'oi— Maui is the best!

69

ARLENE, ARLEEN are favorite Irish names meaning a pledge. German variations of this name are ERLINE, ERLEEN, IRMA, and ERMA. 'ŌLELO PA'A is Hawaiian for an oath or promise.

ARNOLD is from the Old High German and means strong as an eagle or literally eagle rule—a name indicating great power. There are no eagles in Hawai'i, however there is a hawk, the 'IO. IKAIKA ME HE 'IO would mean strong as an 'IO (the Hawaiian hawk).

ARTHUR, ART. This name has several meanings from several different languages: Celtic, strong as a rock, noble; Welsh, bear-hero; and Norse, Thor's eagle. King Arthur was the legendary King of England who ruled Camelot and established the Knights of the Round Table. For the the Hawaiian we have chosen a word that combines several of this name's meanings. 'IO LANI means majestic hawk (there were no Hawaiian eagles). This beautiful hawk is found only in the high forests on the Island of Hawai'i.

ASHLEY is from the Old English and means from the ash tree lea or meadow. In Hawaiian we would have MAI KE KULA for from the meadow.

AUDREY is from the Germanic and means noble. This is the original form of the more modern name ETHEL. In Hawaiian LANI was the word for sky and also a word that was used to refer to the chiefs and nobility.

AUGUST, AUSTIN, and the feminine form AUGUSTA are from the Latin and mean exalted and majestic. This is another name that like AUDREY could be LANI in Hawaiian; another appropriate Hawaiian word could be KILAKILA meaning majestic and strong; having poise that commands admiration.

AURORA is Latin for the dawn. In Roman mythology Aurora was the goddess of the dawn. In Hawaiian the light of early dawn is ALAULA. Seldom does the Hawaiian word come so close in sound to the English—a happy coincidence for this lovely name.

AVA, AVIS means bird in Latin. The Hawaiian for bird is MANU. In Hawaiian there is a saying—He manu hulu—a feathered bird is a prosperous person, and He manu hulu 'ole—a featherless bird is an impoverished person.

The Hawaiianized-English of AVA is AWA a native Hawaiian word meaning a port or harbor.

BALDWIN is from the Teutonic and means bold or noble friend. This was a very popular name during the Crusades. In Hawaiian the expression LAWAKUA which means strong-backed or muscular has come to mean a person who is a dear friend or noble companion.

BARBARA is from the Greek and means stranger or literally a barbarian. When the barbarians invaded ancient Greece they spoke a language that the Greeks could not understand. To imitate these barbarians, the Greeks said 'baa baa'— thus our words babble, barbarian, and strangely enough this popular name. MEA 'E is an appropriate Hawaiian equivalent for BARBARA. It means extraordinary, unusual, strange, wonderful, and stranger—one of another race.

The Hawaiianized-English form of BARBARA is PALAPALA—a post-contact Hawaiian word which means a document of any kind.

BARNABY and the variant BARNEY are Biblical in origin from the Hebrew language and honor St. Barnabus who journeyed with St. Paul on his first mission. The meaning is son of consolation. The rather lengthy Hawaiian equivalent of this name would be KEIKI KĀNE (son) O KA HŌ'OLU'OLU-'ANA (consolation, comfort).

BARRY is from the Old Celtic and means spear and was used to refer to a good marksman. In ancient Hawai'i the spear was used not only as a weapon in war-time, but also during sport contests of spear throwing. Also, various spears were used in catching fish. The sport of spear throwing and the god of spear fighters was LONO-MAKA-IHE.

The Hawaiianized-English form of BARRY is PALI which is also the native Hawaiian word for a cliff.

BARTHOLOMEW and its shortened form BART are Hebrew names meaning son of the furrows, a farmer or ploughman. A rather rowdy event in merrie olde England was the Bartholomew Fair to benefit St. Bartholomew's Hospital in London. The Hawaiian word for farmer is MAHI'AI.

The Hawaiianized-English form of BART is PALAKA which is also the native Hawaiian word meaning indifferent.

BEATRICE and the variations BEA and TRIXIE are from the Latin and mean she who blesses. In Hawaiian KAI HO'OPŌMAIKA'I would mean one who blesses since the word PŌMAIKA'I means to bless or cause good fortune.

The Hawaiianized-English form for BEA is PEA which is the Hawaiianized form of the English word for a fair or carnival; for TRIXIE the Hawaiianized-English form is KALIKA, a Hawaiianized form of the English word silk.

BECKY. See REBECCA

BELINDA is from the Germanic and Italian and literally means like a serpent, or wise and immortal. In ancient times the serpent symbolized both wisdom and long life. An appropriate Hawaiian word for this name might be IHU-PANI which means an expert or wise person. The literal meaning is closed (pani) nose (ihu). It is thought that IHUPANI came to mean a wise person because it referred to the ability to dive deeply and hence to profound knowledge.

BELLA and **BELLE** are from the Latin and mean the beautiful one. In Hawaiian KA NANI means the same thing.

We would caution you not to use the Hawaiianized-English form of this name which is PELA since this is also the Hawaiian word for fertilizer.

BENEDICT and its variations BENNETT, BENSON, DIXIE, and DIXON are all from the Latin and mean spoken well of or blessed. The word benedict means a newly married man, especially one who has been a confirmed bachelor but has changed his mind. Two Hawaiian possibilities exist for this name: 'ŌMEA which means a beloved or respected person, or PŌMAIKA'I which means blessedness.

BENJAMIN and the variants BEN, BENNY, and BENJY are all from the Hebrew and mean son of the right hand or fortunate. In Hawaiian the word PŌMAIKA'I means fortunate, blessed, prosperous.

The Hawaiianized-English form of BEN is PENI, which is also the Hawaiian transliteration of the English word pen.

BENNETT. See BENEDICT

BENSON. See BENEDICT.

BERNARD and the feminine forms BERNADINE and BERNADETTE are all from the Teutonic and mean stern bear or resolute commander. The bear, the largest and strongest animal in Northern Europe, was regarded in ancient times as sacred. The Hawaiian word 'ALIHIKAUA means commander in battle.

BERNICE is from the Greek Nike, the goddess of victory. In Hawaiian LANAKILA means victory.

BERT. SEE BERTRAM, BURTON, ROBERT.

BERTHA is from the Old High German and means the bright, beautiful and glorious. In Hawaiian NANINANI means beauty, glory, and splendor. To intensify the meaning of a word the Hawaiians would frequently duplicate it, so NANINANI just makes NANI doubly beautiful and bright!

The Hawaiianized-English form of BERTHA is PELEKA, which is also the Hawaiianized word for an English surveying term, the perch.

BERTON. See BURTON.

BERTRAM and the shortened form BERT are from the Teutonic and mean bright raven or illustrious. The raven was, in ancient times, a highly esteemed bird. Although there are no Hawaiian ravens, there is a magnificent Hawaiian crow, the 'ALALĀ, now very rare and found only on the Big Island of Hawai'i. The word 'ALOHI means bright and splendid, so by combining 'ALALĀ 'ALOHI we have bright raven.

The Hawaiianized-English form of BERT is PELEKA, for the meaning, see Bertha.

BERYL is the Greek for a beautiful blue-green gemstone. Beryls, the gems, are not found in Hawai'i. For a Hawaiian equivalent we have chosen MEA MAKAMAE meaning precious object or treasure.

BESS, BETH, BETSY, BETTY. See ELIZABETH.

BEVERLY and its shortened form BEV are Anglo-Saxon and refer to someone from the town of Beverly in Yorkshire England. The name literally means dweller at the beaver's meadow. There were no beavers in ancient Hawai'i. Probably the first contact the Hawaiians had with this animal was in the hats of stylish Europeans so they invented the term 'Īlio-hulu-pāpale (dog-fur-hat) for this animal! Perhaps a Hawaiian equivalent of this name could be a shorthand form— MEA NOHO KULA—dweller at the meadow.

73

BIANCA. See BLANCHE.

BLAINE is from the Anglo-Saxon meaning to bubble or flame; or from the Celtic meaning the lean one. In Hawaiian ULA means to flame (this is also the Hawaiian lobster). MĀPUNA is the Hawaiian for a bubbling spring.

The Hawaiianized-English form of BLAINE is PALAINA which is also a native Hawaiian word meaning turning away in embarrassment.

BLAIR is from the Celtic and means plain or level land. KULA means plain, open country.

The Hawaiianized-English form of this name is PALAILA which is also a native Hawaiian word meaning over-ripe as bananas.

BLAKE is an Anglo-Saxon occupation name; a blake was someone who bleached linens—the name has come to mean fair-complexioned. In Hawaiian KEA means white or fair-complexioned. In ancient Hawai'i people with fair complexions were often favorites at the royal court. The Hawaiians did not have woven fabric, clothing was made from the pounded bark of the wauke or paper mulberry tree and called kapa. A person who would bleach and dry the tapa was called KAI KI'OLENA.

BLANCHE and **BIANCA** (an Italian form) have their origin in the Old High German. Both mean white and fair, or bright and shining. In Hawaiian A'IA'I means bright as moonlight, fair, white, and clear. WAHINE 'ILI A'IA'I meant a woman with skin fair and clear (see also BLAKE).

BONNIE is a popular Scottish name that means sweet, fair, lively, graceful and good. The Hawaiian word MAIKA'I means good, beautiful and righteous.

The Hawaiianized-English form is PONI which is also a native Hawaiian word meaning to anoint.

BOYD is from the Celtic and means light-haired. A small number of the ancient Hawaiians had a red tinge to their hair and these people were called 'EHU. It is an anthropological mystery how these people with reddish hair came to be a part of the dark-haired Polynesian race. The only other light hair known to the Polynesians was the gray hair of old age and this was called PO'O HINA or PO'O KEA.

BRADLEY and the shortened form BRAD are Anglo-Saxon in origin and mean from the broad meadow.

74

MAI KE KULA ĀKEA is the Hawaiian, KULA meaning the plain or open country.

BRADY is an Anglo-Saxon place name and means from the broad island. The Hawaiian word for island is MOKU, therefore, MAI KA MOKU ĀKEA would mean from the broad island.

If your name is BRADY you would probably not want to use the Hawaiianized-English form of your name— PALAKA, since this is also a native Hawaiian word mean- ing indifferent or careless.

BRAM. See ABRAHAM.

BRANDON is Teutonic in origin meaning from the flaming hill. This is likely a variant of BRENDAN, the Irish sea-faring saint. A feminine variant may be BRENDA. In Hawaiian MAI KA PU'U ULA AHI would mean from the flaming (ULA AHI) hill (PU'U).

BRANDY is not a traditional name but it has recently become popular. BRANDY would have its origin in the Dutch word 'branden'—to burn and now refers to an intoxicating liquor made by distilling wine. For the Hawaiian of this name we have chosen WAI (water) AHI (fire). Fire water is a popular way of describing intoxicating liquor and is a much better choice than PALANI—the word the Hawaiians chose to describe brandy when it was introduced into the Islands. PALANI is an ancient word meaning among other things 'to stink'. PALANI was also used to describe the French or a Frenchman. It was the French who introduced brandy to the Islands.

BRENDA and the masculine form BRENDAN are from the Celtic and mean sword blade or flame. AHI is the Hawaiian word for fire; an ardent lover was called an IPO AHI (firey sweetheart). The Hawaiian goddess of fire was PELE (out of respect to the goddess the Hawaiians did not use this name unless it was revealed in a dream). Another Hawaiian form for this name could be KILA meaning knife blade, KILA also means strong or bold.

BRENT is from the Anglo-Saxon and means a steep hill. KAHAKEA is a poetic form used to refer to a high chief and means high, inaccessible as a cliff.

BRETT is a French name and means a native of Brittany. There is no Hawaiian equivalent for this name. Perhaps the closest we can come would be the Hawaiian term KAMA'ĀINA which means child of the land or native son. The original meaning of this name would indeed have referred to a native son or a child of the land of Brittany.

If your name is BRETT you would not want to use the Hawaiianized-English form of this name which is PALEKA since it is also the Hawaiianized form of the Biblical word meaning a carbuncle!

BRIAN and its variant forms BRYAN and BRYANT are both from the Celtic and Gāelic and mean strong and mighty leader. In Hawaiian 'ALIHIKAUA means a commander in battle.

BRIDGET, BRIDGETTE is from the Gāelic and means the strong. BRIDGET was the Irish goddess of wisdom, fertility, forestry, and fire. One Hawaiian form might be KILAKILA which means majestic, strong, having the poise that commands admiration; another could be HAUMEA who in Hawaiian legends was the earth-mother goddess and the great source of female fertility.

BROOK or **BROOKE** are forms of a surname that have, in modern times, become popular as given names. The meaning is naturally a brook or stream. In Hawaiian WAIKAHE is a stream, literally meaning flowing water.

BRUCE is a Scottish name borrowed from the French and it signifies a woods. Scotland's national hero is Robert Bruce who secured the independence of the country in the 14th century. This name has been very popular in Scotland ever since. In Hawaiian NAHELE means a forest or grove of trees.

BRUNO is a Germanic name which comes to English via the Italian. It means dark or of brown complexion. 'ILI KOU means dark-skinned, or having skin as dark as the wood of the kou tree. The beautiful wood of the kou tree was very valuable to the ancient Hawaiians.

BURTON and its variants BURT, BERTON, and BERT are English place names meaning a town on a hill. The variant BURT can also be Germanic and means bright, clear, and excellent. The Hawaiian equivalent to town (KŪLANAKAUHALE) on a hill (PU'U) is the rather lengthy KŪLANAKAUHALE MA LUNA O KA PU'U. For BURT we would choose 'ALOHI which means bright, brilliant.

76

BYRON is an Anglo Saxon name meaning bear, and therefore, strong. It is also an English place name meaning from the bower or cottage. For the Hawaiian we can use IKAIKA meaning strong and powerful. In the Hawaiian language a word was often repeated to form a new word with special emphasis.

CADDIE. See KATHERINE.

CALVIN is from the Latin and means bald. In Hawaiian KAMANI KE PO'O is a poetic way of referring to a bald person. In ancient Hawai'i the wood of the KAMANI tree was used for calabashes. This hard wood was polished to a smooth shiny finish, thus PO'O (head) smooth and shiny like the KAMANI refers to a bald person.

The Hawaiianized-English form of this name is KALAWI-NA which is also the Hawaiianized word for a person of the Calvinist religion.

CAMERON is a Celtic name meaning crooked nose. Originally the family name of a Scottish clan, this name has become popular as a given name. In Hawaiian IHU KAPAKAHI would be the translation of this name. IHU means nose and also means kiss since it was the ancient Hawaiian custom to touch noses in greeting; KAPAKAHI means crooked and lop-sided.

CAMILLA, CAMILLE is from the ancient Etruscan language and means a noble maiden of fine character. For the Hawaiian we have chosen KA LANI PŪLOKU. PŪLOKU means comely and tender as a young maiden or virgin, a second meaning for this word is bright and sparkling as the sun or dew so this one word combines two attractive meanings for this name. LANI is the Hawaiian word for heavenly and is also used to refer to the royalty or ALI'I.

CANADACE and it shortened form CANDY are from the Latin and Greek and signify fire-white or glowing. LIHOLIHO is a Hawaiian word meaning very hot, firey, glowing. This name is also associated with royalty as the popular name for King Ka-mehameha II and Ka-mehameha IV (Alexander Liholiho).

CARA is an Irish pet name meaning dear one. It has also become a popular Italian name. There can be no nicer Hawaiian translation for this name than KE ALOHA—the beloved. In the Hawaiian language ALOHA is the word for love, mercy, kindness. It is a wonderful compliment to say a person has ALOHA or behaves with ALOHA.

The Hawaiianized-English form of this name is KALA which is the native Hawaiian word for to loosen or untie.

CARINA and the variants CAREEN, CARIN, CARINNA, CARYN all find their origin in the Latin word meaning the keel. In Hawaiian IWI KA'ELE means keel. IWI literally means bones. In ancient Hawai'i, the bones of the dead were considered very sacred, thus there are many Hawaiian expressions with IWI taking on the meaning of 'life'.

The Hawaiianized-English of this name is KALINA which is a native Hawaiian word meaning a waiting.

CARL, CARLA, CARLOTTA, CARLY. See CHARLES.

CARMEN and **CHARMAINE** are from the Latin and mean a song. A closely related name may be CHARMIAN, possibly from the Greek meaning joy. In Hawaiian a song or chant is a MELE; the word MELE is also the Hawaiianized-English form of merry and has become quite popular in the expression 'Mele Kalikimaka'—Merry Christmas.

CAROL is from the Old French and means to sing joyfully. This name could also be a variant of the masculine CHARLES. An appropriate Hawaiian equivalent is KANI LE'A which means to sing cheerfully, as the birds.

CAROLINE, CAROLYN and its shortened forms CARRIE, CARY, and CARLY are possible variants of the Teutonic CHARLES (which see), or CAROL, described above.

The Hawaiianized-English of CARRIE, and CARY is KALI which means to wait or hesitate; the Hawaiianized-English of CARLY is KALALI which could mean KA (the) LALI (greasy one).

CARSON is a Scandanavian family name, son of CAR, now being used as a given name. The meaning of the name is of the marsh or brush land. In Hawaiian MAI KA 'ĀINA ULUEKI would be the equivalent of this name. (ULUEKI meaning brush or undergrowth).

CASSANDRA and the shortened forms CASS and CASSIE are from the Greek and refer to a prophetess-princess of Troy whose warnings were never believed. The meaning is helper of men. In Hawaiian KŌKUA means helper and comforter.

CATHERINE and the shortened form CATHY are from the Greek and mean pure. The name was originally spelled with a K, however, when the name reached England centuries ago, the initial letter was changed to C. In Hawaiian MA'EMA'E means pure, attractive, and chaste. (see also KATHERINE)

You would not want to use the Hawaiianized-English form of CATHERINE which is KAKALINA, since this is also the Hawaiianized-English word for gasoline! The Hawaiianized-English form of CATHY is KAKA which means in Hawaiian to rinse clean (beware KĀKĀ meaning to excrete).

CECIL and the feminine form CECELIA are from the Latin and mean the dim-sighted or blind. This is an ancient Roman clan name and possibly recalls an ancestor who was blind. The Hawaiian for blind is MAKA PŌ which is literally MAKA (eye) and PŌ (night).

The Hawaiianized-English form of CECIL is KEKILA which could be a combination of the native Hawaiian words, KE (the),and KILA (high place); the Hawaiianized-English form of CECILIA is KIKILIA which is also the Hawaiianized- English word used for the southern part of Italy, Sicily.

CELIA and its variants CELINE, the Italian and French form CELESTE, and CELESTINA / CELESTINE are from the Latin and mean heavenly. In Hawaiian LANI is the word for heavenly and is also a word used to refer to a very high chief.

CHAD is from the Celtic and means a warrior. It is from the Celtic word 'cad' meaning a battle. A suitable Hawaiian equivalent would be KOAPAKA which is an ancient word which means valiant and brave, especially in battle.

CHANTAL, CHANTEL, CHANTELLE, and SHANTEL are modern names which could have their origin in the French place name Chantal. There was a French saint, St. Jean de Chantal. The name ultimately would mean a stony place. This name is not used in France. The Hawaiian form would be KŪLANA PŌHAKU; KŪLANA (place) and PŌHAKU (stony).

CHARLEEN, CHARLOTTE. See CHARLES.

CHARLES is an ancient Germanic name with numerous variations. Some of the masculine forms are: CARL, KARL, and the short form CHUCK; some feminine forms are CARLA / KARLA, CARLOTTA, CHARLA, CHARLOTTE, and CHARLEEN

/ CHARLENE / SHARLENE. This name means man or strong; the feminine forms mean royal. It has been a royal name since the time of Charlemange (Charles the Great). The Hawaiian word for man is "kāne". "Kāne", with the capital "K", however, is the great god KĀNE. KĀNE was one of the four leading Hawaiian gods—the god of creation. It might be a bit presumptuous for a mere mortal to use this name. Therefore, other choices for both the masculine and feminine forms of this name could be KILAKILA which means strong, majestic, having poise that commands admiration or, LANI meaning heavenly and also referring to members of the royal class.

Hawaiianized-English forms which are also native Hawaiian words include: CHARLES = KALE which means watery; CARL/KARL and CARLA/KARLA = KALA which means to loosen or untie.

CHARMAINE. See CARMEN.

CHÉRIE is the French word for darling, sweetheart, and cherished one used as a given name. A possible variant would be the mis-spelling CHERRY, based on the French pronunciation, further variations would be the popular CHERYL and CHERYLLYN. There would be several Hawaiian possibilities— MAKAMAE (precious, of great value, highly prized, darling); MILIMILI NANEA (a cherished person that absorbs and delights one); or even LEI since this word also is used to refer to a beloved person or sweetheart, a less formal form might be HUAPALA which means sweetheart in the sense of 'sweetie-pie'.

CHESTER sometimes shortened to CHET is from the Old English and means from the Roman camp. This is an English place name that we see in the name of the city of Manchester. In Hawaiian MAI KE KAHUA means from the camp, with KAHUA being an open place or flat place suitable for camping.

The Hawaiianized-English form for CHET is KEKA which is a modern Hawaiian word for the English word sex or gender.

CHLOE is from the Greek and means the young grass or a blossom. In Hawaiian PUA is the word for a blossom or flower and also refers to the tassel of the sugar cane, a giant member of the grass family. MOHALA another possibility means blooming, or the unfolding of a flower's petals.

80

CHRISTIAN and the feminine variations CHRISTA, CHRISTINA, CHRISTINE, CHRISTIE, CHRISTY, KIRSTEN, KIRSTEEN, KIRSTY, and TINA are all from the Greek and refer to a follower of Christ, the Greek meaning of the word is the anointed. In Hawaiian MEA LA'A means the consecrated or holy one.

The Hawaiianized-English form of TINA is KINA, which is also the Hawaiianized word for China and Chinese.

CHRISTOPHER and its short form CHRIS are from the Greek. The meaning is Christ- bearer. In Christian legend CHRISTOPHER was a ferryman who carried the Christ- child across a rampaging river. St. Christopher has become the patron saint of travellers. For the Hawaiian we have chosen 'IMI LOA which means seeker or distant traveller and also is used to mean one with deep knowledge.

The Hawaiianized-English form of CHRIS is KILIKA which is the modern Hawaiian word for silk.

CINDY. This name is a shortened form of CYNTHIA or LUCINDA. LUCINDA is the feminine form of LUCIAN.

CLARENCE and the more popular feminine forms of this name; CLARA, CLARE, CLAIR (which is also used for boys in France), CLARICE, CLARINDA, and CLARISSA are all from the Latin and mean clear, bright, illustrious. 'ALOHI is the Hawaiian word which means bright and splendid.

CLARK is from the Latin and Anglo-Saxon. This name meant the person was a clerk, usually a priest, scholar, or member of the clergy. Since members of the clergy were better educated than the general populace this name came to mean learned. In Hawaiian the word NA'AUAO means learned and intelligent.

The Hawaiianized-English form is KALAKA which could also be equivalent to the native Hawaiian KA (the) LAKA (tame).

CLAUDE and the feminine forms CLAUDIA, CLAUDETTE, and CLAUDINE are derived from the name of an ancient Roman patrician family. It is said to be connected with the Latin word cladus which means lame. In old Hawai'i the ALI'I were the patricians or royal families. 'O'OPA is the Hawaiian word for lame or a lame person. Another more appealing form for this name would be MAULIAUHONUA

81

which means descendant of old high chiefs of a land; ancient as a an established family.

CLAYTON and the shortened form CLAY are Old English place names and mean a dweller in a town built near a clay pit. A partial Hawaiian equivalent for this name could be MA'A'ULA'ULA which means red clay. 'ULA'ULA means red and also sacred or royal, most likely because red was considered a chiefly color.

CLEMENT and the feminine CELEMENTINE are from the Latin and mean mild and merciful. The Romans had a goddess, Clementia, worshipped as the goddess of Pity. The Hawaiian word ALOHA has as one of its many meanings to show kindness and mercy, so ALOHA could be used for this name. In ancient Hawai'i LONO-I-KE-AWEAWE-ALOHA (Lono with small streaks of affection) was a god of mercy and also a love-making god!

CLEO is from the Greek and is a shortened form of CLEOPATRA which means fame (cleo) of her father (patra). In Hawaiian KAULANA means famous, celebrated, and renowned.

CLIFFORD, CLIFTON, CLINTON, and the abbreviated CLIFF and CLINT are all Old English place names and mean ...... near the cliff. CLIFFORD is stream or crossing near the cliff, CLIFTON and CLINTON are town near the cliff. In Hawaiian PALI is a cliff; ALA'AU is a stream crossing, and KAUHALE is a town, PILI I KA PALI is near the cliff. Another, simpler possibility would be HALEHALE which means high and towering as a cliff.

The Hawaiianized-English form of CLIFF is KALIPA which is the Hawaiian form of the English word caliph.

CLIVE is a name closely related to the CLIFF...names. It is also from the Old English and means a cliff. The Hawaiian would be PALI.

CLYDE is a Scottish place name from the River Clyde. As the River Clyde flows past Scotland's red sandstone cliffs it is quite red and murky. In Hawaiian 'ŌMEA means reddish and murky. Additionally, 'ŌMEA means a beloved and respected person.

The Hawaiianized-English of this name is KALIKE which could be equivalent to the native words meaning KA (the) LIKE (similar).

COLLEEN in Irish is a girl. In Hawaiian the word PŪLOKU means comely and tender as a young girl and also bright, sparkling, as sun or dew. Another possibility would be MAKA LEHUA which literally means the petals of the lehua and was a term used to describe something lovely and attractive, most often young girls.

The Hawaiianized-English form of this name is KALINA, which could in native Hawaiian words, mean KA (the) LINA (soft, sticky)—not a very attractive equivalent for this name!

COLIN and the feminine COLLETTE are possibly French pet names derived from NICHOLAS which means victory. They may also be associated with the word columba—dove from the Latin via Scottish. The Hawaiian word for victory is LANAKILA. For the feminine COLLETTE we could use NŪNŪ MAKA ONAONA, which means soft-eyed dove—a term of endearment.

CONRAD is from the Germanic and means able in speech and counsel. In Hawaiian POHOKANO means able counselor.

CONSTANCE and its more popular shortened form CONNIE is a Latin virtue name and means constant. In Hawaiian KŪPA'A means steadfast, constant, and loyal.

The Hawaiianized-English form of CONNIE is KONE which is also the Hawaiianized word for an animal appearing in the Bible, the rock badger.

CORA, CORETTA and the French form CORINNE are derived from the Greek and mean a maiden. In Hawaiian PŪLOKU means comely and tender as a virgin and also bright, sparkling as sun or dew. (see also COLEEN)

The Hawaiianized-English form of CORA is KOLA. This is an especially inappropriate name for a maiden since in native Hawaiian KOLA means rigid, sexually excited, especially in terms of the male anatomy!

CORAL is from the Greek and Latin and refers to the red coral found in the Mediterranean. In Hawaiian PUNA is the word for coral. HINA-(I)-KE-KĀ, the goddess of canoe bailers was considered to be 'the mother of the corals.'

COREY, CORY is a Scottish place name meaning ravine, mountain glen. In Hawaiian 'ŌPAKA means a mountain ravine.

CORNELIA and the seldom used masculine CORNELIUS are from Latin for the cornel tree, known as the dogwood in the United States. In Victorian England each flower had a meaning. In this special language of the flowers the cornel means duration. LI'ULI'U means in Hawaiian to pass much time, a long time.

COURTNEY is from the Old English and is a variant of COURTLAND which means from the court land. MAI KA 'ĀINA ALI'I would be the Hawaiian equivalent for this name, 'ĀINA = land, and ALI'I = royal.

CRAIG is from the Celtic and means a stony hill. In Hawaiian a hill is PU'U and stony is PŌHAKU so we would have PU'U PŌHAKU for CRAIG.

CRYSTAL was originally a Scottish diminutive of CHRISTOPHER but is now more closely associated with the rock crystal used in jewelry. HUAKA in Hawaiian means clear as crystal, dazzling.

The Hawaiianized-English form of CRYSTAL is KIKALA which is also the Hawaiianized form of a Biblical word for a fir or pine tree.

CURTIS and **CURT/KURT** are from the Old French and mean courteous. In Hawaiian WAIPAHĒ means courteous and gentlemanly.

CYNTHIA and its popular shortened form CINDY are from the Greek. Mount Cynthus in Greece was regarded as sacred to the goddess Artemis—the goddess of the moon, thus this name is associated with this goddess. In ancient Hawaiian legends HINA is the goddess of the moon. MAHINA means both the moon and moonlight.

DAISY is from the Old English and means the day's eye because this flower with its brilliant yellow center and white petals resembles the sun—the eye of the day. In Hawaiian MAKA LENA is the yellow center of a flower like the daisy. (You might like to know that MAKA LENA also means an unfriendly, suspicious glance from under the eyelid! The word MAKA has as one of its many meanings eye) So, perhaps you might prefer NA'ENA'E which is the name for native Hawaiian daisies and also means fragrant for this name.

DALE is a name that can be used for both boys and girls. It is from the Old English and means a dweller in a valley.

84

In Hawaiian MEA NOHO I KE AWĀWA would mean dweller in (MEA NOHO I) the valley (KE AWĀWA).

The Hawaiianized-English form of this name is KAILA which is the Hawaiianized form of the English word style.

DAMIEN is the French form of DAMON which means the tamed or taming. In Greek legend DAMON pledged his life for his friend Pythias, so this name has become a synonym for a loyal friend. In Hawaiian HOALOHA or HOA ALOHA means a friend and beloved companion, and LAKA means to tame.

DANA is from Scandanavian mythology. The name meant mother of the gods; a more modern meaning is bright as day. DANA is another name that can be used for both boys and girls. In Hawaiian mythology HAUMEA is the earth-mother goddess and mother of the volcano goddess Pele. 'ALOHI is the word for bright, shining as in the phrase " 'Alohi e like me ka lā i ke awakea"—as bright as the sun at noon.

The Hawaiianized-English form is KANA which is a native Hawaiian word meaning to count in tens.

DANIEL and the shortened forms DAN, DANNY, and the feminine DANIELLA, DANIELLE are all from the Hebrew and mean God is my judge. The rather lengthy Hawaiian equivalent would be 'O KE AKUA KA'U LUNA KĀNĀWAI. The concept of a judge (LUNA KĀNĀWAI) was introduced to Hawai'i by the Western world along with the concept of written laws.

DAPHNE is from the Greek and means the laurel tree. The MAILE is a native Hawaiian vine with shiny fragrant leaves. Like the laurel, garlands (leis) were made of MAILE as tokens of esteem; MAILE was especially cherished by hula dancers since it was believed to be the embodiment of Laka, goddess of the hula.

The Hawaiianized-English form of DAPHNE is KAPANA which is a native Hawaiian word meaning edge or boundary.

DARLENE. See DARYL.

DARREN, DARIN are variations of the Persian DARIUS which means a man of many possessions, wealthy. In Hawaiian the phrase KI'I MAKA NUNUI was used to describe a wealthy and important person. The phrase literally means big eyed image. In the ancient Hawaiian religion the KI'I were the images of the gods.

The Hawaiianized-English form of DARREN is KALINA which could be a combination of the native Hawaiian words KA (the), and LINA (soft, sticky).

DARYL, DARRYL, and **DARREL** are sometimes used for both boys and girls; all of these, and the definitely feminine form DARLENE are from the Old English and mean darling, or tenderly beloved. In Hawaiian MAKAMAE is a precious thing of great value, darling; MILI NANEA is a cherished person that absorbs and delights.

DAVID, and its shortened forms DAVE, DAVEY are from the Hebrew and mean beloved. In Hawaiian HIWAHIWA means precious and beloved.

The Hawaiianized-English form of DAVID is KAWIKA. KAWIKA has become such a popular name that many people now think it is actually a Hawaiian name!

DAWN is the Scandanavian form of Aurora—the dawn and means to grow light in the morning. In Hawaiian mythology HINE-'EA was the goddess of the sunrise. The phrase KA 'ULA WENA means the rosy glow of sunrise; and ALAULA means the light of early dawn.

The Hawaiianized-English form is KANA which is a native Hawaiian word meaning to count in 10's.

DEANNA, DEANNE. See DEAN and DIANE.

DEAN, the Italian DINO and the feminine forms DEANNIE and DEE are all variations of DALE.

The Hawaiianized-English form of DEAN is KINI, a native Hawaiian word which means a multitude; of DINO it is KINO, a native Hawaiian word which means body.

DEBRA, DEBORAH and the popular shortened form DEBBIE are all from the Hebrew and mean bee, the queen bee. In ancient times it was thought the bee could foretell the future and in ancient Egypt, the bee signified royal power. In Hawaiian NALO MELI is the word for the honey-bee. NALO (a small insect) plus MELI (honey); the queen bee would be NALO MELI MŌ'Ī WAHINE.

DEIDRE, DEIRDRE is a Celtic name and means sorrow. In an Irish romance it was prophesied that DEIDRE would bring ruin to Ireland. In Hawaiian MINAMINA means regret and sorrow and to prize something greatly, especially something in great danger of being lost.

DELLA and **DELIA** are Greek in origin and mean from the Island of Delos. The name Delos comes from the Greek word for ring, because Delos is surrounded by a ring of other small islands. In Hawaiian LEI MOKU would be a lei or circle of islands.

The Hawaiianized-English form KELA, is a native Hawaiian word meaning excelling.

DENIS, DENNIS, DION, DIONNE, and the feminine DENISE are from the name of the Greek god of wine Dionysius. In ancient Greece the festival of Dionysius was held each year in the fall to celebrate the grape harvest. In ancient Hawai'i there was a similar harvest festival called the MAKAHIKI. MAKAHIKI was celebrated with the bringing of gifts of produce to the chiefs, games, and the suspension of wars and kapus. In Hawaiian the word HIWAHIWA means festive and also precious and beloved.

The Hawaiianized-English form of DENIS is KENIKA which is the word the Hawaiians used for the English game of tennis.

DEREK, DERRICK, DIRK are variants of a Germanic name meaning the people's ruler. In Hawaiian ALI'I is ruler and KANAKA is mankind, so we would have ALI'I O KE KANAKA.

DESIRÉE is from the Latin and French and means exactly what one would expect— the desired. In Hawaiian MAKAKĒHAU means the heart's desire, and 'ANO'I means desired one or beloved.

DESMOND is from the Celtic and means man of the world. This name may also mean man from Munster—the Irish province. It is an old Irish clan name. The Hawaiian equivalent would be KĀNE O KA HONUA.

DEVIN is from the Celtic and means a poet. In Hawaiian HAKU MELE meaning a weaver of songs would be closest to this name.

DEXTER is from the Latin and means right hand or on the right. In Hawaiian LIMA 'ĀKAU means right hand or dependable helper.

DIANA, DIANE, DIANNE, and the variants DEANNA and DEANNE (which may also be associated with the name

DEAN) are all from the Latin and refer to DIANA the Greek goddess of the moon. In the ancient Hawaiian religion HINA was the goddess of the moon. MAHINA means the moon and also moonlight, and KŌNANE is bright moonlight.

DICK. See RICHARD.

DINA, DINAH are from the Hebrew and mean the judged. In the Bible Dinah was the daughter of the prophet Jacob and his wife Leah, and according to Biblical legend DINAH was very beautiful. The Hawaiian equivalent would be MEA I HO'OKOLOKOLO'IA.

The Hawaiianized-English form of DINA is KINA which is also the Hawaiianized word for China and Chinese.

DION, DIONE. See DENIS

DIXIE, DIXON. See BENEDICT.

DOLORES and its shortened forms DORI, DORY, and DORRIE are all from the Latin and mean sorrow. In Hawaiian MINAMINA means regret and sorrow; to prize something greatly, especially something in great danger of being lost.

The Hawaiianized-English form of DORI, DORY, and DORRIE is KOLI which is a native Hawaiian word meaning to whittle.

DOMINIC and more popular French feminine form DOMINIQUE are from the Latin and mean belonging to the Lord. This name was frequently bestowed on a child born on Sunday—the Lord's day. After the introduction of Christianity in Hawaii the word LĀPULE was invented to mean Sunday—it is a combination of LĀ (sun) and PULE (prayer).

DONALD and the shortened forms DON and DONNIE are from the Celtic and mean proud chief or prince of the world. In Hawaiian ALI'I is chief and HA'AHEO is proud and haughty, thus we would have ALI'I HA'AHEO, another possibility would be HE ALI'I HOLO'OKO'A meaning a chief over all or supreme.

The Hawaiianized-English for DON would be KONA which is a native Hawaiian word referring to the leeward side of the Hawaiian Islands.

DONNA is a Latin nobility name and literally means Lady. In Hawaiian LANI was a word used to refer to persons who were members of the ali'i (chiefly) class. LANI also means heavenly.

The Hawaiianized-English form of DONNA is KONA (see DONALD).

DOREEN is from the French and means golden. In Hawaiian PALA LUHIEHU means golden yellow, a beautiful yellow.

DORINDA is a 16th century literary name related to DOROTHY and has the same meaning.

DORIS and the possible shortened forms DODI and DORI are from the Greek and mean of the sea. In ancient legend DORIS was a sea goddess and the mother of 50 nymphs. In ancient Hawai'i, HALE-LEHUA was a sea goddess who lived in the depths of the channel between O'ahu and Kaua'i. The name literally means Lehua- blossom house.

The Hawaiianized-English form of DODI is KOKI, a native Hawaiian word which means snub-nosed.

DOROTHY, DOROTHEA and its variations DORA, DOLLY and DOT are all from the Greek and mean gift of God. This name is the feminine form of Theodore, originally the word elements were in reverse giving us THEODORA. In Hawaiian MAKANA LANI meaning heavenly gift would be an appropriate equivalent for this name.

The Hawaiianized-English form of DORA is KOLA, a native Hawaiian word which means hard, rigid, and sexually excited.

DOUGLAS and the abbreviated form DOUG are from the Scottish and mean dark blue water. In Hawaiian ULIULI means the dark blue of the sea.

DREW. See ANDREW.

DUDLEY is an Old English place name which simply means a place. In Hawaiian KŪLANA is the word for a place or site and also means outstanding and prominent.

DUKE is from the Latin and means a leader. The Hawaiian word for a leader or commander is ALAKA'I.

The Hawaiianized-English form of DUKE is KUKE, a native Hawaiian word which means a nudge or push.

DUNCAN is from the Celtic and means brown warrior or one with a dark complexion. In Hawaiian KOA 'ILI KOU would mean KOA (warrior) and 'ILI KOU (dark complexion).

DUSTIN is from the Germanic and means a brave warrior or fighter. In Hawaiian the word KOA means both brave and a warrior. The koa tree is the largest of the native Hawaiian forest trees and is prized for its beautiful and strong wood.

DWAYNE and its alternate spelling DUANE are from the Celtic name DOANE which means from the dunes or a poem or song. In Hawaiian MELE is a song or chant; MAI NĀ PU'E would mean from the dunes.

DWIGHT is from the Germanic and means white light. In Hawaiian AO means light, daylight and KEA means white so we would have AO KEA.

DYLAN is from the early Welsh signifying the sea or god of the waves. In Hawaiian KE KAI means simply the sea and NALU KAI means the waves of the sea.

EARL, ERROL and the feminine EARLENE, EARLINE stem from one of the oldest Anglo-Saxon nobility names meaning noble man or chief. In Hawai'i the royal or chiefly class was called the ALI'I and AUALI'I means royal and chiefly. Another word referring to royalty was LANI a name of great antiquity which designates high honor.

EARTHA is from the Anglo-Saxon and means exactly what we would expect—the earth. It is from an older Teutonic name for the earth-mother goddess. In the ancient Hawaiian religion HAUMEA was the earth-mother goddess. HAUMEA literally means 'red ruler'. The color red was considered a sacred color.

EDGAR is from the Anglo-Saxon and means happy warrior. In Hawaiian KOA refers to a brave, fearless soldier; and HAU'OLI means happy so we would have KOA HAU-'OLI for this name.

EDITH/EDYTH and the variation ARDITH with the shortened form EDIE are ancient Anglo-Saxon names meaning prosperous war or rich gift. In Hawaiian PŌMAIKA'I means fortunate and prosperous.

EDMOND, EDMUND. See EDWARD.

EDNA is from the Hebrew and means pleasure and delight. In Hawaiian 'OLI means joy and pleasure; in the Hawaiian language a word was frequently repeated to intensify the meaning, for example 'OLI'OLI could be used for EDNA.

EDWARD, EDMOND, EDMUND, and the short forms ED, EDDIE, and NED are all from the Anglo-Saxon and mean prosperous guardian. In Hawaiian KAHU is the word for guardian and LAKO means rich and prosperous so the combination of KAHU LAKO would give us prosperous guardian.

The Hawaiianized-English form of NED is NEKE which is a native Hawaiian word for a tropical fern.

EDWIN and the feminine form **EDWINA** are from the Anglo Saxon and mean wealthy friend. In Hawaiian, friend is HOALOHA and wealth is WAIWAI so the combination HOALOHA WAIWAI would mean wealthy friend. A single Hawaiian word combining both these meanings would be 'AIKAPA meaning a privileged friend who shares in the profits of a friend's land.

EILEEN, AILEEN, and **ELAINE** are Gāelic forms of a word meaning pleasant or overjoyed. In Ireland this name is used as a substitute for the Greek HELEN which means the bright one. In Hawaiian LA'ELA'E is a word which combines both the Gāelic and Greek meanings. LA'ELA'E means bright, serene, calm and pleasant, and is also the name of a star.

The Hawaiianized-English of AILEEN and EILEEN is AILINA which could be a combination of the native Hawaiian words AI = sexual relations and LINA = sticky!

ELEANOR, ELEANORE, ELINOR, and some of its shortened forms ELLIE, LENA, NELL, NELLY, and NORA are all variations of the Greek HELEN which came to England via France. Its meaning is the bright one. In Hawaiian KE 'ALOHI is the splendid, shining, and brilliant. There are many other Hawaiian possibilities a few of which are: LINO (or LINOLINO) meaning bright, shining with splendor; LILE (or LILELILE) meaning bright, shining, dazzling; NALE (or NALENALE) meaning clear and bright.

The Hawaiianized-English form of LENA is LENA which is also a native Hawaiian word meaning yellowish, as with jaundice.

ELIZABETH and its numerous variations, some of which are: BESS, BETH, BETSY, BETTY, ELSIE, ELIZA, LIBBY, LISA, LIZA, LIZZIE, TESS are all from the Hebrew and mean oath of God. El is Hebrew for God. In Hawaiian HO'OHIKI A KE AKUA would be an literal translation for this name.

The Hawaiianized-English form of BESS, TESS, and BETH is PEKA a native Hawaiian word which means to tattle or tell tales; BESTY and BETTY become PEKE which means a dwarf or elf.

ELLA is from the German and means all. In Hawaiian PAULOA means all, everything.

ELLEN, ELENA are more variations of the Greek HELEN which means light, the bright one. ELLEN is an Early English form of HELEN. The Hawaiian form would again be KE 'ALOHI—the splendid, shining, and brilliant. For additional Hawaiian possibilities see ELEANOR.

ELROY is from the French and means the king. In ancient Hawai'i KE ALI'I would mean the chief; in the modern days of the monarchy KE MŌ'Ī would mean the king.

ELSA and the variants ELSIE, and ILSA are from the Old German and mean a noble maiden. In old Hawai'i LEILANI was a name used to signify a royal child (the literal meaning is heavenly lei). In modern Hawai'i LEILANI is very popular name for girls.

ELVA. See ALFRED.

ELVIRA is from the Latin and means white or fair. In old Hawai'i a poetic term for a person with fair skin was 'ILIPUAKEA—'ILI (complexion) PUAKEA (the tint between white and pink as in the clouds at sunset).

EMILY and its variants AMELIA, MEL, MELLIE, and MILLIE are the feminine forms of the less common masculine EMIL, all are from the Latin or Germanic. The Latin stems from the name of a Roman clan 'Aemilius'; the Germanic stems from a word meaning industrious. In Hawaiian PA'AHANA means industrious and hard-working.

EMMA is Germanic and is derived from the name of an ancient Teutonic hero. The name can mean a nurse or ancestress. In the ancient Hawaiian religion the goddess HAUMEA and her husband Wākea are considered the ancestors of all Hawaiians. The Hawaiian word KUPUNA means an ancestor, usually a grandparent and also means the starting point or source.

ENID is from the Welsh and means life or soul. A heroine in Arthurian legend was called ENID. She represented all that is noble and true in womanhood. In Hawaiian MAULI means life, heart, and seat of life.

92

ERIC, ERIK, RICK and the feminine forms ERICA, ERIKA are from the Scandanavian and mean ever-ruling and regal. In Hawaiian PALI LOA means a distant or lofty cliff and is used figuratively to mean regal and aristocratic.

ERIN is from the Gāelic and is the name for Ireland and also the name of a legendary queen. The word ERIN in the Irish language means peace. In Hawaiian MALUHIA means peace, calm. The word MALUHIA was used to describe the solemn awe and stillness that reigned during some of the taboo ceremonies in ancient Hawai'i.

ERLENE, ERLINE. See ARLENE.

ERMA. See ARLENE.

ERNEST, ERNST and the feminine ERNESTINE are from the Germanic and mean vigor or intent. In Hawaiian IKAIKA means vigorous and strong.

ERROL. See EARL

ESTELLE. See STELLA.

ESTHER is from the Persian and means a star. It could also be a variation of Ishtar—the Babylonian goddess of love. In Hawaiian the word HŌKŪ means star.

ETHAN is from the Hebrew and means steadfast. In Hawaiian 'ONIPA'A means immovable and steadfast. 'ONIPA'A was the motto of both King Ka-mehemeha V and Queen Lili'u-o-ka-lani.

ETHEL is from the Germanic and means noble. The Hawaiian word LANI means royal and high born; PO'IU means of high rank, glorious.

EUGENE, GENE and the feminine forms EUGENIA, EUGENIE are from the Greek via Latin and mean well-born and noble. For the masculine of this name AUALI'I royal and chiefly could be used; for the feminine PUALANI, descendant of royalty (literally heavenly flower) would be suitable.

The Hawaiianized-English form of GENE is KINI which is a native Hawaiian word meaning a multitude.

EVA, EVE, EVELYN, EVALINA, and **EVONNE** are all from a Hebrew word meaning life. Adam called his wife EVE because she was to be the mother of all human life. In the ancient Hawaiian religion HAUMEA was the mother of all Hawaiians. The Hawaiian word OLA means life.

93

The Hawaiianized-English of EVA, EVE is IWA, which means nine or ninth. 'IWA is a name for the great frigate bird and also means thief because the frigate bird steals his food from other birds.

EVAN is possibly the Welsh equivalent of JOHN or a Celtic word for youth or one who is well born. The Hawaiian word LIKO combines both meanings of this name since LIKO meaning a newly opened leaf was figuratively used to mean a youth, especially the child of a chief.

The Hawaiianized-English form of EVAN is EWA a native Hawaiian word which means unstable.

EVELYN. See EVA.

FAITH, FAY, FAYE are all virtue names from the Latin meaning faithful. It is also possible that FAY may be either a shortened form of FAITH or the word FAY which means a fairy. MANA'O'I'O is the Hawaiian for faith. PUA is a word which usually means a blossom but it is also the name of a mischievous goddess of sorcery—about the closest the Hawaiians came to fairies.

FAY, FAYE. See FAITH.

FELIX and the feminine forms FELICIA and FELICITY which are more popular today are from the Latin. FELICITAS was the Roman goddess of good luck. In Hawaiian PŌMAIKA'I means good fortune and prosperity.

FIONA is from the Irish and means the white or the fair. In Hawaiian KEA means white, clear; a fair-complexioned person.

FLORENCE and its variants FLORA, FLO, FLOSSIE, FLORINDA are all from the Latin. FLORE was the Roman goddess of flowers and springtime. In Hawaiian KUPULAU is the spring season, the meaning is literally 'leaf sprouting'.

The Hawaiianized-English form of FLO is POLO which is a native Hawaiian word meaning large, plump, and fat.

FLOYD. See LLOYD.

FORD is a surname that is sometimes used as a given name. It is from the Teutonic and means a river crossing. In Hawaiian ALA'AU means a river ford or crossing.

FRANCIS and its shortened form FRANK and the numerous feminine variations which include FRANCES,

FRANCINE, FRANCESCA (the Italian form), the French FRANCQISE, and the shortened forms FANNY and FRANNY all mean free. These names come from the name of an ancient Germanic tribe that settled in the land that came to be named after them—France. In Hawaiian KŪ'OKO'A means free and independent.

The Hawaiianized-English forms which are the same as native Hawaiian words are as follows: FRANCES, FRANCIS is PALAKIKA, PALA = ripe and KIKA = sticky; FRANK is PALANI which is the surgeon fish, but which also means stinky! FANNY becomes PANE which means an answer or reply.

FRANKLIN is from the Germanic and means a free man. In Hawaiian KUĀKAHI means free of interference and also unmarried. It could be that the Hawaiians were on to something here!

FREDERICK, FRED, and the Germanic FRITZ along with the feminine forms FREDA, and FREDERICA all stem from the Old High German word for peaceful. This is derived from an old Teutonic name for the goddess FREYA who we recall every week on Friday (FREYA'S-day). In Hawaiian MALUHIA is one word for peace and serenity; another would be LA'IKŪ meaning great calm, peace, and serenity.

GABRIEL the feminine GABRIELLE and the shortened form GABBY are from the Hebrew and mean God is mighty. IKAIKA LOA KE AKUA is the Hawaiian equivalent, IKAIKA LOA = mighty and KE AKUA = God.

GAIL. See ABIGAIL and GALE.

GALE was originally a masculine name but is now used for both sexes. It and the variants GAYLE and GAIL have several meanings from several sources. From the Norse this name could mean to sing; from the Irish it could mean a stranger; and from the Scandanavian it could mean a ravine. It is also possible that the form GAIL is simply a shortened form of ABGAIL. In Hawaiian MELE is to sing or chant; MEA 'Ē is a Hawaiian word for stranger—its full meaning is extraordinary, unusual, strange, wonderful, and stranger— one of another race.

The Hawaiianized-English form of this name is KAILA which is the name of a native Hawaiian tree.

GALEN is from the Latin and means sea calm. In Hawaiian MALINO means calm, quiet,as the sea.

95

The Hawaiianized-English form of GALEN would be KALENA which is a native Hawaiian word meaning to stretch, as the hide of an animal.

GARETH, GARTH, GARRETT and **GARY** are Anglo-Saxon warrior names going back to the days of knighthood. They mean powerful with the spear. GARTH may also be an Anglo-Saxon occupation name meaning gardener. In ancient Hawai'i the art of spear throwing was LONO-MAKA-IHE named for the god of spear throwers, LONO MAKA IHE (literally spear point LONO).

The Hawaiianized-English form of GARY is KALI, a native Hawaiian word which means to wait or to loiter; GARETH is KALEKA, which could be a combination of the native Hawaiian words KA (the) and LEKA (slimy).

GAVIN is a Scottish form of GAWAIN, which means hawk of battle. GAWAIN was one of King Arthur's knights. In Hawaiian 'IO-LANI means royal hawk or hawk of heaven. This was a symbol of royalty and became the name of the Palace of the Hawaiian monarchs.

The Hawaiianized-English form of GAVIN is KALINA, which could be a combination of the native Hawaiian words KA (the) and LINA (sticky).

GAY, GAYLENE, GAYLYNN are all from the French and mean merry. In Hawaiian 'OLI'OLI means happy, gay, and joyful.

The Hawaiianized-English form of GAY is KAI which is the Hawaiian word for sea water.

GENE. See EUGENE.

GENEVIEVE, GUINEVERE and the most popular variant of this name JENNIFER and its shortened form JENNY are all from the Welsh and mean white or fair one. This is no doubt a reference to the ancient goddess of the moon. St. Genevieve (who is the patron saint of Paris) was a shepherd girl who saved Paris from destruction by Attila the Hun. In the ancient Hawaiian religion HINA was the goddess of the moon; LAMALAMA refers to a person of fair complexion and also means bright, animated and vivacious. A'IA'I means bright as moonlight, fair, and brilliant, (a woman with skin fair and clear was wahine 'ili a'ia'i).

The Hawaiianized-English form of JENNIFER is KINIPELA. In this case, disregarding the meaning of the Hawaiian language has created an unfortunate combination of two native Hawaiian words, KINI meaning a multitude and PELA meaning fertilizer or decomposing flesh.

GEOFFERY, JEFFERY and the shortened form JEFF are all from the Germanic name GOTTFRIED which means God's peace or the gift of peace. In Hawaiian HO'OMALUHIA means to cause or give peace; MAKANA O KA MALU means gift of peace.

GEORGE and the feminine variations GEORGIA, GEORGETTE, GEORGINE, GEORGINA are from the Greek and mean a tiller of the soil or farmer. St. George is the patron saint of England. In Hawaiian MAHI'AI is a farmer.

The Hawaiianized-English form of GEORGE is KEOKI which has become one of the most popular Hawaiianized-English names.

GERALD, GERHARD, JERROLD and the feminine form GERALDINE are all frequently shortened to JERRY. The masculine is from the Teutonic and means spear-rule or brave warrior. The feminine form was invented by the Earl of Surry who in his love poems to Lady Elizabeth Fitzgerald called her 'my fair Geraldine.' In Hawaiian KOA means both brave and warrior. For the feminine 'ILIPUAKEA is a poetic term for a person with a fair complexion—'ILI (complexion) PUAKEA (the tint between white and pink as in the clouds as sunset). This Hawaiian poetic term seems a good choice for 'my fair GERALDINE'.

GERMAINE is from the Latin via French and means a German, another possible meaning is neighbor. The Hawaiian for a neighbor is HOA ALOHA; HOA means a companion or friend.

GERTRUDE and the shortened forms TRUDIE and TRUDY are from the Germanic language and mean spear-strength. GERTRUDE was the name of one of the Norse Valkyries, goddesses who carried slain heroes from the battlefield to heaven. In Hawaiian IHE is a spear and KAUILA is a hard dark wood that looks like mahogany and when polished was the preferred wood for making the strongest spears. Thus IHE KAUILA would come closest to the meaning of this name.

GIAN, GIOVANNI. See JOHN.

GILBERT is from the Germanic via the French and means bright pledge or bright sword. In Hawaiian HO'OHIKI 'ŌLINO means bright ('ŌLINO) pledge (HO'OHIKI),and IHE AHI means a firey (AHI) sword (IHE).

GILLIAN. English form of JULIANA; see JULIAN.

GINA. See REGINA.

GINGER is possibly a pet form of VIRGINIA but more likely a flower name—the fragrant ginger blossom. In Hawaiian 'AWAPUHI is the wild ginger and 'AWAPUHI- KE'OKE'O and 'AWAPUHI-MELEMELE are the fragrant gingers used in making leis.

GINNY. See VIRGINIA.

GLADYS is possibly a Welsh form of CLAUDIA or a name derived from a Celtic word meaning princess. In Hawaiian LEILANI is a royal child, thus a princess. LEILANI literally means heavenly lei; another possibility would be KA-MU'O-O-KA- LANI which literally means the young leaf bud of heaven and refers to the child of a chief.

GLEN, GLENN and the feminine forms GLENNA, GLENDA and GLYNIS are Celtic place names and mean from the valley or glen. MAI KE AWĀWA would be the Hawaiian for this name.

GLORIA, GLORIANA are from the Latin and mean glorious. GLORIANA is a combination of GLORY and ANN and could be glorious grace. In Hawaiian both HANOHANO and NANI mean glorious and splendid, and ALOHA or MAIKA'I mean grace, so for GLORIANA we could have ALOHA NANI.

GOLDA, GOLDIE are from the Anglo-Saxon and mean golden. PALA LUHIEHU means golden-yellow, a beautiful yellow.

GORDON is an Anglo-Saxon place name meaning round hill. Originally this was the name of a great Scottish clan so there is also the suggested meaning of hero or strong man. In Hawaiian ME'E is a hero; PU'U POEPOE would be round hill (PU'U is a hill).

GRACE is from the Latin 'gratia' and means grace, favor, and thanks. The Hawaiian word ALOHA brings together all these meanings.

GRAHAM is an Old English residence name meaning from the gray home or home. It is also the name of a distinguished Scottish clan with a suggested meaning of warlike. In Hawaiian MAKEKAU is warlike, and HALE is home. So from the gray home would be MAI KA HALE 'ĀHINAHINA.

GRANT is a French variation of grand or great. Its simple Hawaiian equivalent is NUI which means great.

GREGORY, GREG is from the Greek and means watchful. In Hawaiian MAKA'ALA also means watchful—MAKA (eyes) and ALA (awake).

GRETA, GRETCHEN are both Germanic forms of MARGARET which means the pearl. In Hawaiian MOMI is the pearl.

The Hawaiianized-English of GRETA is KALEKA which could be a combination of a native Hawaiian words KA (the) and LEKA (stick, slimy).

GUINEVERE see GENEVIEVE.

GUY is French meaning a guide or Germanic meaning woods. In England Sir Guy was one of King Arthur's knights. In Hawaiian ALAKA'I is a leader or guide.

The Hawaiianized-English form of GUY is KAI which is the Hawaiian word for sea water.

GWENDOLYN and its more popular shortened forms GWEN and WENDY are all from the Welsh and mean white circle—this is most likely a reference to the ancient goddess of the moon. In the ancient Hawaiian religion HINA was the goddess of the moon and MAHINA is the word for the moon; KŌNANE means bright moonlight.

The Hawaiianized-English form of GWEN is KAWENA which could be a combination of the native Hawaiian words KA (the) and WENA (glow).

HAMILTON is from the Old French and means from the mountain hamlet (town). In Hawaiian we would have MAI KA NOHONA I UKA or, more simply, MAUKA meaning from the uplands.

HANNAH is from the Hebrew and means grace. This is the Latin and Greek form of ANNA. In Hawaiian MAIKA'I means goodness and grace.

The Hawaiianized-English of HANNAH is HANA, a native Hawaiian word meaning work. One of Hawai'i's favorite expressions is "Pau hana"—to finish work.

HANS, see JOHN

HARLEY is an Anglo-Saxon place name and means from the meadow. In Hawaiian MAI KE KULA would mean the same thing.

HAROLD and the shortened form HAL are from the ancient Anglo-Saxon and are names long associated with warriors, the meaning would be mighty in battle. The ancient Hawaiian word KOAPAKA means valiant and brave, especially in war.

The Hawaiianized-English of HAL is HALA a native Hawaiian word meaning sin, error, offense.

HARRISON is from the Old English and means son of HENRY. In Hawaiian KAMA KĀNE or KEIKI KĀNE means a male child or son. (see also HENRY)

HARRY, HANK. See HENRY.

HARVEY, HERVEY are from the Old French and mean bitter or from the Celtic meaning flourishing; another possible meaning is battle-worthy. 'AWA in Hawaiian is the kava plant. A narcotic beverage was made from the pulverized roots of this plant, because of kava's bitter taste this also became the word for bitter. The Hawaiian for flourishing, and luxuriant is LUPALUPA, and KAUA KŪPONO would be battle-worthy.

HAZEL is an Anglo-Saxon plant name meaning commander. Among the old Anglo-Saxon tribes carrying a hazel tree wand was a symbol of authority. In Hawaiian 'ALIHIKAUA means a commander in battle.

HEATHER is a Middle-English flower name and refers to the heather shrub. 'ŌHELO is a Hawaiian plant in the same botanical family as heather. The 'ŌHELO is a small shrub with edible red berries that taste something like cranberries. The Hawaiians considered the 'ŌHELO sacred to the goddess Pele and made offerings to her by throwing branches with berries into the volcano at Kī-lau-ea.

HEIDI. See HILDA.

HELEN, HELENA, HELENE, ELLEN, ELAINE (see also EILEEN and ELEANOR), are but a few of the world-wide variants of this ancient name. HELEN is from the Greek word 'ele' mean-ing light, and thus this name means the light or bright one. In the ancient world HELEN of Troy symbolized female beauty in its most perfect form. KE 'ALOHI means the bright, the splendid and the glittering one. (for additional Hawaiian forms see ELEANOR).

The native Hawaiian word HELENA means going.

HELOISE. See LEWIS.

HENRY, HARRY, HANK and the feminine variants HARRIET, HENRIETTA are from the Germanic and mean ruler of the home. The name HARRY comes from a mispronun-ciation of the French HENRI. ALI'I O KA HALE is an exact Hawaiian translation of this name. Interestingly, the Hawaiianized-English form of HARRY is HALE, the native Hawaiian word for house and home.

HERBERT, HERB is Germanic and means the bright warrior. KOA is one word for warrior and 'ALOHI for bright, thus we would have KOA 'ALOHI.

HERMAN is from the Old High German via Latin and Anglo-Saxon and means man of the army, a soldier or warrior. The name of one of Hawai'i's strongest and most beautiful native trees is the KOA which is also the word for a warrior.

HILARY is from the Latin and means cheerful. It is from the same Latin word from which we have taken the word hilarious. This is one of the few names still used in modern times for both boys and girls. HOIHOI means both cheerful, joyful and amused.

HILDA and the variant HEIDI are from the Old German and mean battle. HILDA was the name of the chief of the Valkyries (goddesses of the battlefield) in Scandanavian mythology. In ancient Hawai'i certain women called KOA WĀHINE (warrior women) or WĀHINE KAUA (battle women) were taught the skills of warfare. Although they did not usually fight they would rush to the aid of a warrior in danger and were even known to take the place of their husband if he was killed in battle. In Hawaiian both KAUA and PAIO mean battle.

HIRAM is from the Hebrew and means most noble and exalted. PALI LOA means in Hawaiian a distant cliff but also has the meaning of aristocratic and noble.

HOLLY and the seldom used masculine HOLLIS are from the Anglo-Saxon holly plant. In ancient times the evergreen holly was associated with winter festivals, and in Christian times it came to be associated with Christmas. Holly signifies good luck. In Hawaiian PŌMAIKA'I means fortunate and lucky.

The Hawaiianized-English form of HOLLY is HALI which is a native Hawaiian word meaning to carry.

HOPE is a virtue name meaning just what it says. It was first used by the Puritans in the 17th century. MANA'OLANA is hope in Hawaiian.

HORACE, HORATIO, and the feminine HORATIA are all from the name of a Roman tribe and the possible meaning is keeper of the hours. The original form of this name was HORATIUS, the name of many Roman heroes. In Hawaiian KIKO LĀ means timekeeper, the literal meaning day marker.

HOWARD is from the Germanic and means a strong mind or watchman. In Hawaiian NO'ONO'O LAWA would be strong or wise mind and KAHU would be a watchman.

The Hawaiianized-English of HOWARD is HAOA which means in Hawaiian to be branded, or a sour stomach.

HUBERT is from the Germanic and means bright mind. The Hawaiian equivalent could be MANA'O AKAMAI, a combination of MANA'O (mind, thought) and AKAMAI (wise) which together means spirit of wisdom.

HUGH and HUGO are from the Germanic and mean intelligent. NA'AUAO means intelligent in Hawaiian.

The Hawaiianized-English of HUGH is HIU a native Hawaiian word which means to throw or fling violently.

HUMPHREY is a Germanic name meaning keeper of the peace. In Hawaiian MALU is peace and MĀLAMA is to care for, so this name would be MĀLAMA O KA MALU.

HYACINTH is in Greek mythology the beautiful youth HYACINTHUS who was killed accidentally. Each year Apollo, the sun god, caused Hycinthus to be re-born in the form of this beautiful spring flower which bears his name. This name is now exclusively a girl's name. In the language of the flowers the white hyacinth means unobtrusive beauty. A Hawaiian equivalent could be NOHEA meaning lovely.

IAN see JOHN

IDA has several possible sources and meanings. From the Teutonic word for to work hard or woman (an apt description of the life of most women throughout history!!); or from the Norse goddess Iduna—the goddess of spring. In Hawaiian the spring season was KUPULAU which literally means leaf sprouting.

ILSA. See ELSA.

IMOGENE is a name that came into being because of a printer's error. In Shakespeare's play "Cymbeline" the heroine was to be INNOGEN but was printed IMOGEN which could mean last born, youngest child or an image. KA MULI LOA is the very last child, the youngest in Hawaiian.

INES, INEZ is a Spanish form of AGNES.

INGRID, INGA, INGE are from the Scandanavian legend of Ing's ride. Ing was the god of fertility and prosperity. Each year in the spring he took a ride astride his golden boar. The boar's tusks plowed the earth into furrows for spring planting. In the ancient Hawaiian religion HAUMEA was the goddess of fertility.

IRA is the Hebrew for watchful, a watcher. MAKA (eyes) and ALA (awake) makes the word MAKA'ALA which means in Hawaiian watchful and alert; careful—MAKA'ALĀ = blind!!

The Hawaiianized-English of IRA is IWA, the native Hawaiian word for the number nine.

IRENE is from the Greek 'Eirene' which means peace and is also the name of the goddess of peace. MALUHIA means peace and serenity in Hawaiian, and LA'IKŪ is quiet, great calm and serenity.

IRIS is from the Greek word for a rainbow. The goddess IRIS was the personification of the rainbow who carried messages across her many colored bridge from the gods to man. In Hawaiian ĀNUENUE is a rainbow.

IRMA is from the Latin and Teutonic and means noble. LANI is the Hawaiian word for heavenly and also a person of noble birth.

IRVIN, IRWIN, and **IRVING** have two possible origins— from the Gāelic meaning handsome or from Norse mythology meaning sea friend because warriors who fought at sea

103

were so called. NOHEA is handsome and of fine appearance in Hawaiian, and HOALOHA KAI or MAKAMAKA KAI
would be sea friend.

ISABEL, ISABELLA, BELLA, BELLE are French variants of
ELIZABETH.

ISSAC is from the Hebrew word for laughter. In the Bible
Sarah and Abraham were promised a son in their old age.
When the child was born Sarah laughed with joy, thus the
child was called ISSAC. In Hawaiian 'AKA is laughter.

IVAN is a Russian form of JOHN.

IVY in the language of the flowers signifies faithfulness.
In Hawaiian KŪPA'A means loyal and faithful.

JACK. See JACOB

JACOB is a name derived from the Hebrew which has
become much more popular in its Latin form of JAMES.
Other variants of this name are JAKE, JACK, JACKIE, JIM,
JAMIE and the French JACQUES and JOCK. From the French
we have the feminine form JACQUELINE. Recently the
Spanish form of JAMES which is JAIME (sometimes spelled
JAMIE) has become popular as a girl's name. The Biblical
origin of this name is from JACOB of the Old Testament. The
name means supplanter or following after because JACOB
was born after his twin Esau. In Hawaiian UKALI means to
come after or follow.

The Hawaiianized-English form of JACK and JOCK is
KEAKA which is also the Hawaiianized form of the English
word theater. The Hawaiianized-English form of JAMES and
JIM is KIMO. KIMO is one of the most popular Hawaiianized-
English names. The ancient Hawaiians had a game called
KIMO, similar to the English game of 'jacks'.

JACQUELINE. See JACOB.

JAIME, JAMIE. See JACOB.

JAMES is a form of JACOB.

JAN, JANE, JANET, JANETTE, JANICE, JANINE, JANIS are
all feminine forms of JOHN.

JARED and **JARROD** are from the Hebrew and mean the
descending or descendant. PUKANA is the Hawaiian for a
descendant and also means a remembrance.

JASMINE is from the Arabic name YASMIN. It is a flower name for the fragrant jasmine. JASMINE flowers (and peacocks) were favorites of Princess Ka-'iu-lani at her estate in Wai-kiki. The Hawaiians created the word PĪKAKE for both the peacoks and the jasmine flower—Ka-'iu-lani's favorites.

JASON is from the Greek and means the healer. One of the most popular stories of ancient times is the quest of JASON for the Golden Fleece. In Hawaiian MA'I- OLA was a god of healing (the name literally meaning cured sickness). Another healer of ancient Hawai'i was the KAHUNA LAPA'AU, literally a curing expert who knew the secrets of herbal remedies.

JAY as an independent name is from the Anglo-Saxon. It is a bird name and possibly refers to the crow. JAY is also a shortened form of many other names. There is a rare Hawaiian crow called the 'ALALĀ, a word which means to caw or crow.

The Hawaiianized-English form of JAY is KEI, a native Hawaiian word meaning to glory in.

JAYNE could be another variation of JOHN or, a more romantic possibility, it could be derived from the Sanskrit for victory. In Hawaiian LANAKILA is victory.

JEAN, JEANNE, JEANETTE are more variations of JOHN from the French form JEAN, JEANNE. JEANNE D'ARC (JOAN of Arc) is a French national heroine.

JED is from the Hebrew and means beloved of the Lord. MEA HIWAHIWA O KA HAKU is a possible Hawaiian form with HIWAHIWA meaning precious or beloved.

JEFFERY, JEFF. See GEOFFERY.

JENNIFER, JENNY see GENEVIEVE.

JEREMIAH and **JEREMY** are related Hebrew names meaning God will uplift, or exalted by the Lord. JEREMIAH was one of the great prophets of the Old Testament. One possible Hawaiian equivalent would be AMOAMO KE AKUA, or more simply HO'OHANOHANO meaning to honor, exalt and glorify.

JEROME and a shortened form it shares with several other names—JERRY are Greek meaning holy name. INOA 'ALA means esteemed name and was used in Hawai'i especially when referring to the name of a chief.

JERRY. See JEROME, GERALD.

JESSE is from the Hebrew. In the Bible JESSE is the father of King David of Israel; the name seems to mean the Lord is. In Hawaiian KA HAKU means simply the Lord. There is no direct Hawaiian equivalent for the English word "is".

JESSICA and the shortened form JESSIE are from the Hebrew and mean God is looking or riches. In medieval times this was almost exclusively a Jewish name. In Hawaiian KŪʻONOʻONO means wealthy or well-to-do, and NĀNĀ KE AKUA would mean God is looking.

JEWEL is from the Latin meaning a precious stone. In Hawaiian MEA MAKAMAE means a precious object or treasure.

JILL is the English diminutive of GILLIAN which in turn comes from JULIA, a feminine form of JULIAN.

The Hawaiianized-English form of JILL is KILA, a native Hawaiian word which means a high place.

JIM. See JACOB.

JOAN, JOANN, JOANNE, JOHANNA, JOJO are all feminine forms of JOHN.

JOCELYN and **JOYCE** are names with two possible origins: Old German meaning descendant of the Goths, or from the Celtic meaning champion. These were both boys names until the late 1800's, now they are more popular for girls. In Hawaiian POʻOKELA means the best or a champion.

JODIE, JODY. See JUDITH.

JOEL, JOELLE are from the Hebrew and mean Jehovah is the Lord. In Hawaiian this would be ʻO IĒHOWA KA HAKU, obviously a modern equivalent since the Jehovah of the Bible was unknown to the ancient Hawaiians.

JOHN is from the Hebrew and means God is gracious. Throughout history and around the world this name and its many variations has been one of the most popular ever names for both boys and girls. There are at least 100 masculine variations of JOHN and most likely an equal number of feminine variations. The following partial list covers only the most popular. Masculine: IAN (Scottish), JAN (Dutch), SEAN, SHAUN, SHAWN, SHANE (Irish); EVAN (Welsh); HANS; IVAN (Russian); JEAN (French); GIAN, GIOVANNI (Italian); JOHANN (German); JUAN (Spanish). Feminine: JAN,

JANE, JANET, JANETTE, JANICE, JANINE, JANIS, JEAN, JEANNE, JEANETTE, JOAN, JOANN, JOANNA, JOANNE, JOHANNA, JOJO, JUANITA, and SIOBHAN-an Irish form of JOAN.

The Hawaiian form of this name could be LOKOMAIKA'I KE AKUA; AKUA is the word for God and LOKOMAIKA'I means good, generous, gracious and kind.

The Hawaiianized-English forms of those names which have Hawaiian meanings are as follows: JAN = KANA which means by tens; JANE, JEAN, and JEANNE = KINI which means a multitude; JOJO = IOIO, round grooves in carving. A special caution with JOJO since the Hawaiian 'O'TO'O also means clitoris. The Hawaiianized-English form of JEANETTE is KINIKA and of JUNANITA is WANIKA. The former is also the Hawaiianized form of the English word ginger, and the latter the Hawaiianized form of varnish. The Hawaiianized-English form of JOHN is KEONI which has become a very popular name.

JOLIE, JOLINE are from the French and mean pretty. In Hawaiian NANI means beautiful, pretty and glorious.

JONAH, JONAS are from the Hebrew and refer to the dove, a symbol of peace. MANU KŪ is the term the Hawaiians invented for the European dove. MANU is a bird and KŪ the sound of a dove. MALUHIA is a Hawaiian word for peace.

JONATHAN is a variation of NATHANIEL.

JORDAN is from the Hebrew and means descending. In Hawaiian IHO means to descend or go south before the wind.

JOSEPH, the feminine form JOSEPHINE, and the shortened forms JO and JOE are all from the Hebrew meaning increase or addition. This name is from the Biblical story of Rachel and Jacob who gave this name to their first son with the hope that they would be adding future children to their family. In Hawaiian HO'ONUI is to increase and multiply.

JOSHUA, JOSH are from the Hebrew and mean the Lord saves. The Hawaiian equivalent of this name would be HO'ŌLA KA HAKU.

JOY is a virtue name that was popular with the Puritans and its meaning is to rejoice and be joyful. In Hawaiian HAU'OLI is happy and joyful.

JOYCE. See JOCELYN.

JUAN and **JUANITA** are Spanish forms of John.

JUDITH and the shortened forms JUDY, JODIE, and JODY are all from the Hebrew. The original meaning of this name is a woman of Judea, hence a Jewess. However, in modern times it has come to mean praise or praise the Lord. In Hawaiian MILILANI is to praise and exalt.

The Hawaiianized-English form of JODY is KOKI, a native Hawaiian word which means snub-nosed, as a bull-dog.

JULIA, JULIE, JULIET. See JULIAN.

JULIAN is a name with numerous variations. All stem from the Roman family name Julii. This family was originally noted for its members long hair. In time the name came to mean hairy or downy and then acquired the meaning youthful, possibly because of the relationship of down and young birds! In Hawaiian PŪNUA is a young bird or fledgling, it also has the additional meanings of a youth or sweetheart. Some of the variations of this name are: JULIUS, JULES and the feminine forms: JULIA, JULIANA, JULIET, JULIETTE, JULIE, JILL,and GILLIAN—an English form.

The Hawaiianized-English form of JULES is KIULE which is also the Hawaiianized form of the English word jury; JILL = KILA, a native Hawaiian word which means a high place.

JUNE is a name referring to the month of June. This name is quite recent, its earliest recorded use is in the 20th century. In Hawaiian HINAIA-'ELE'ELE corresponds to the last part of the month of June and is also the name of a star.

JUSTIN, and the feminine JUSTINE, JUSTINA are from the Latin and mean the just or honest. In Hawaiian KŪPONO is just, fair, and honest.

KAREN is the Danish form of KATHERINE. The Hawaiianized-English form is KALENA which could be a combination of two native Hawaiian words, KA (the) and LENA (yellowish).

KARL, KARLA see CHARLES.

KATHERINE is a name with many variations some of which are: KATHRYN; the Irish form, KATHLEEN; the Scottish form, KATRINA and its diminutive TRINA; and the shortened forms CADDIE, KATE, KATHY, KAY, KITTY. All originate from the Greek and mean pure, clean. St. Katherine of Alexandria was an Egyptian princess who was tortured with a spiked wheel for her defense of Christianity. Today there is a rotating firework called the Catherine wheel which recalls her sufferings. In Hawaiian MA'EMA'E means clean and pure.

The Hawaiianized-English forms which correspond to native Hawaiian words are: KAY is KEI which means dignified and glorious; KATHY is KAKI which means cross and irritable; KITTY is KIKI which is a piece of wood used to repair canoes. The Hawaiianized-English form of KATHLEEN and KATHERINE is KAKALINA which is also the Hawaiianized form of the English word gasoline!

KEITH, a popular Scottish name, is said to be similar to the old Gaelic for 'wood'. It is also the name of a line of ancient Scottish earls and might signify wind swift. For the Hawaiian we have MAKANI-KE-OE. This name seems to combine both the Scottish and Gaelic meanings of this name since MAKANI-KE-OE was a Hawaiian wind god who could make plants grow and take the form of a tree.

The Hawaiianized-English form of KEITH is KIKA, a native Hawaiian word which means slippery and slimy.

KELLY, KELLEY is from the Celtic and was originally a family name. It has recently become a popular first name for girls; its meaning is warrior. In Hawaiian a poetic word for a warrior is LEHUA, this word also means a sweetheart and beloved friend and is the name of a native tree with beautiful red flowers.

KELVIN is Gaelic/Irish and means from the narrow river. MAI KE KAHAWAI would mean from the river. In Hawai'i there are very few rivers; because the Hawaiian Islands are relatively new, geologically speaking, all the rivers are narrow!

KENNETH, KEN, KENNY, KENT are Anglicized forms of an old Gaelic name meaning handsome. The first king of Scotland was named KENNETH. In Hawaiian NOHEA is handsome.

KERRY is a Gaelic/Irish name and means the dark one. In Hawaiian we have KA 'ILI KOU which means the dark-skinned one. Literally this means skin like the kou wood. The beautiful kou wood was used by the Hawaiians for cups, dishes, and containers.

KEVIN is an Irish name and means handsome by birth. In Hawaiian NOHEA means handsome and of fine appearance, and NOHEA I KA HĀNAU means handsome by birth.

KIMBERLY, KIM was originally a Celtic surname from the word 'cyn' which means a warrior or chief. In Hawaiian LANI means a very high chief and also heavenly.

The Hawaiianized-English form of KIMBERLY and KIM is KIMO which is the name of an ancient Hawaiian game similar to jacks.

KIRK, KIRBY are from the Gāelic for a church. In Hawaiian HALE PULE, a HALE (house) and PULE (prayer) expresses the idea of a church, a concept which was introduced by the early missionaries. In ancient Hawai'i a HEIAU was a place of worship. Although many HEIAU have been destroyed it is still possible to visit several of these ancient, sacred sites.

KIRSTEN, KIRSTIN, KIRSTY are names the early Greeks gave their daughters in honor of the new Christian religion. For its translation see CHRISTIAN.

KIT see CHRISTOPHER.

KORA. See CORA.

KURT. See CURTIS.

KYLE has two meanings: From the Welsh it could mean narrow channel, and from the Gaelic it could mean handsome. Of course, we will chose NOHEA which is the Hawaiian for handsome.

The Hawaiianized-English form is KAILA which is also the Hawaiianized form of the English word meaning style.

LANA has several possible origins and meanings, including one from the Hawaiian! From the Irish it might mean my child; from the Latin—wool; and in Hawaiian LANA refers to calm still waters and also means floating and buoyant.

LANA, LANE. See also ALAN.

LANCE, LANCELOT is probably a name invented by medieval poets. LANCELOT was the greatest of King Arthur's knights. The meaning of the name is quite naturally lance. In Hawaiian IHE PAKELO is a lance.

LARA is Latin from the Roman gods 'The Lares', household gods who protected the home and fields. In ancient

Hawai'i the family or personal god was called the 'AUMAKUA and was much the same as the Roman Lares. In Hawaiian, the word 'AUMAKUA is also used to describe a trustworthy person.

The Hawaiianized-English for LARA is LALA, a native Hawaiian word which means diagonal.

LAURA is the feminine variant of LAWRENCE. Some of the numerous variations of this name are as follows: LAUREEN, LAUREN, LAUREL, LAURIE, LAURINDA, LOLLY, LORA, LOREN, LORETTA, LORI. All are derived from the Latin city of Laurentis, the so called city of laurels. In ancient times laurel was used as a symbol of victory and victorious athletes were decorated with a wreath of laurel. In ancient Hawai'i the MAILE plant was used in much the same way as laurel. This vine with shiny, fragrant leaves was woven into leis for hula dancers and victorious athletes in the games at Makahiki. Even today to be given a MAILE lei is a great compliment, so MAILE seems a prefect Hawaiian equivalent for LAURA.

The following list gives the Hawaiianized-English forms of the LAURA names which correspond to native Hawaiian words, do note carefully that several of them have highly uncomplimentary meanings: LAURA = LALA which means diagonal; LAURIE = LALI which means greasy as pork fat; LORA = LOLA which means lazy and idle; LORI and LOLLY = LOLI which means to turn or change.

LAVERNE. See VERNON.

LAWRENCE sometimes spelled LAURENCE, the Italian form LORENZO, and the shortened form LARRY have all the same origin as LAURA. Since the Laurel plant is connected with victory LANAKILA, which is the Hawaiian word for victory, could be used for the masculine forms of this name.

The Hawaiianized-English form of LARRY is LALI a native Hawaiian word which means greasy as pork fat!

LEA, LEAH, and **LEATRICE** are all Hebrew Biblical names which mean weary. In Hawaiian LUHI is weary and is also a child tended and raised with devoted care, so perhaps the weariness refers to the parents, rather than the child! In the Hawaiian language LE'A means pleasure, especially sexual gratification and LEA is the goddess of canoe builders and also the name of a star. The placement of the ' is very important! It is thus possible that LEA could be a name like LANA that has an actual Hawaiian meaning of its own.

LEANN. Possibly a combination of LEE and ANN or just another variant of ANN.

LEE, LEIGH is from the Anglo-Saxon and means a meadow. In Hawaiian KULA is open country, meadows, and pastures.

The Hawaiianized-English of LEIGH is LEI, a Hawaiian word know world-wide meaning a garland.

LEIGHTON, an English surname which has become popular as a given name, means one who comes from LEIGHTON—a homestead where leeks were grown. There does not seem to be any Hawaiian equivalent for this name.

LEILA is from the Persian meaning dark-haired or dark as night. It is a name frequently given to a child born at night. In Hawaiian POULI is dark night.

LENA. See HELEN or ELEANOR.

LENORA, LENORE, LEORA are Russian pet forms of ELEANOR.

LEO, LEON, LEONARD, LIONEL, and the feminine LEONA are from the Latin meaning the lion. This is the fifth sign of the Zodiac and according to astrologers gives a lion-like character to those born under this sign (July 22 to August 21). LEONARD is an old German form meaning lion brave. There was no ancient Hawaiian word for lion so the closest we can come is the word LIONA which the Hawaiians adopted from the English for the king of beasts.

LEROY, ELROY, ROY, REX, REGIS are all from the Old French and mean the King. In ancient Hawai'i those of noble rank were the ALI'I; in the more modern days of the monarchy the word MŌ'Ī was used to mean king. The king could therefore be KE ALI'I or KA MŌ'Ī.

The Hawaiianized-English for ROY is LOI which is a native Hawaiian word meaning to look over critically.

LESLIE, LESLEY is a Scottish place name and means the low meadow. In Hawaiian KULA is a meadow and LALO refers to a lower place, thus we would have KULA I LALO.

LESTER is an English place name meaning from the town of Leicester, another meaning is the shining. In Hawaiian KE 'ALOHI is the shining, the splendid.

LETITIA, and its more popular variants TISH, LETTY, and LETA are from the Latin or Spanish and mean gladness or joy. In Hawaiian HAU'OLI means happy, glad, and joyful.

The Hawaiianized-English forms of this name which correspond to native Hawaiian words are: TISH = KIKA which means slippery; and LETA = LEKA which is sticky and slimy. LETTY = LEKI which the Hawaiianized form of the English word lace.

LEWIS, LOUIS, the seldom used form ALOYSIOUS and the feminine forms LOUISA, LOUISE, LOIS, HELOISE, a Germanic form LUANA, and the French form LISETTE are all from the Latin and mean famous in war. LOUIS has been a very popular name in France since early times and many French monarchs had this name. The feminine forms became popular at a much later date. In Hawaiian KAULANA is the word for famous and celebrated, and war would be KAUA, so famous in war would KAULANA I KE KAUA.

The name LUANA is interesting because it is actually a Hawaiian word which means to enjoy oneself, to live in comfort and ease.

LIAM. A pet form of WILLIAM in Ireland.

LIBBY. See ELIZABETH.

LILITH is from the ancient Assyrian and Babylonian languages and means belonging to the night. In Hebrew legend the wife of Adam was LILITH rather than Eve. In Hawaiian POULI means dark night.

LILLIAN, LILA, LILY are of uncertain origin but these names are all connected with the flower—the lily. The lily is a symbol of purity. In Hawaiian MA'EMA'E means pure and attractive. PA'INIU is a native Hawaiian lily with silvery leaves and would be another possibility for this name.

LINDA and the variant LINDY are names with a most interesting ancient German origin. In Old German 'lindi' (this is almost certainly where we get the form LINDY) meant a serpent. In ancient times the serpent was held in awe and worshipped as a symbol of wisdom. Norseman of old, noting the grace and suppleness of serpents, would compliment a beautiful woman by comparing her with a serpent! In more modern times this name has come to be associated with the Spanish word LINDA which means pretty and beautiful. LINDA is now also used as an ending to other names, such as ROSALINDA to mean pretty rose. Since there were no serpents in ancient Hawaiian we can use the Spanish meaning to come to the Hawaiian NANI which means pretty and beautiful.

LINDSAY, LINDSEY is an old English place name which means linden tree island or a hedge. In Hawaiian PILIPĀ means a hedge.

LINDY. See LINDA, MELINDA.

LIONEL is related to LEO (see above) and is a medieval name that was given to one of King Arthur's knights. Its meaning is young lion—LIONA KEIKI.

LISA. Hebrew pet form of ELISHEBA (ELIZABETH).

LISETTE. A French feminine form of LEWIS.

LIZA. Russian pet form of YLIZAVETA (ELIZABETH).

LLEWELLYN may be from the Welsh and mean lion-like, or go back to a more ancient Celtic form meaning leader. In Hawaiian ALAKA'I is leader.

LLOYD is from the Welsh and possibly means gray or brown—this name was used as a title for the sea god Llyr. The best interpretation may be dark complexioned. This name was a favorite with Welsh gypsies. The English, unable to pronounce properly the Welsh double 'l' came up with the variation FLOYD. In Hawaiian 'ILI KOU means dark-skinned, literally skin like the kou wood. The beautiful kou wood was used by the Hawaiians for cups, dishes, and containers.

LOIS. See LEWIS.

LOLA, LOLITA are Spanish diminutives from CARLOTTA and CHARLOTTE, both of which are in turn derived from CHARLES. In Hawaiian LOLA means lazy and idle, or a kind of native fern.

LORILEI is from the German and means the alluring. It is from the name of a steep rock where a beautiful woman (LORILEI) would lure boatmen to their death. In Hawaiian NANI E MAKAHEHI 'IA AI means beautiful and alluring.

LORNA is an invented name created for the late 19th century novel 'Lorna Doone'--the meaning is derived from its association with the old English word lorn meaning lost and forlorn. In Hawaiian NALOWALE is lost and forgotten.

114

LORRAINE is from the old French and means one who comes from the town of Lorraine. We can find no Hawaiian equivalent for this name.

LOUIS, LOUISA, LOUISE. See LEWIS.

LOWELL, LOVELL can be from the Old English and mean the beloved or from the Germanic meaning little wolf. A few of the many ways to say the beloved in Hawaiian are KE ALOHA, 'ŌMEA, and NĒNĒ HIWA.

LUANA. See LEWIS; see also Hawaiian name listing.

LUCAS, LUKE (see also LUCIAN). In the Greek these names would mean man of Lucania. St. Luke was one of the four evangelists and is also the patron saint of doctors. A possible Hawaiian equivalent for this name could be MA'I-OLA, the name of an ancient god of healing. MA'I-OLA means literally, to cure sickness.

LUCIAN, LUCIEN, LUCIUS, LUKE and the feminine variants LUCIA, LUCILLE, LUCINDA (CINDY), LUCRETIA, LUCY are all from the Latin 'lux' meaning light. This was originally a name given to children born at daybreak. In Hawaiian AO is light and also the dawn of day; KA-WENA is the rosy glow of dawn; and HOAKA is bright, shining, to become light.

LULU is a possible diminutive of LOUISE or LUCIA. In Hawaiian LULU means peace, calm, and shelter (as in Hono-lulu—calm harbor).

LYDIA is from the Greek and refers to a girl from Lydia, a district of Asia Minor. There does not seem to be any Hawaiian equivalent for this name.

LYLE and a feminine form LISLE are from the French and mean inhabitant of the island. MEA NOHO MOKUPUNI would be the Hawaiian for this name.

LYMAN is an Anglo-Saxon place name and means from the valley. In Hawaiian MAI KE AWĀWA would mean the same thing.

LYNN, LYNNE is from the Anglo-Saxon and means dweller by a waterfall or pool. The name can be both masculine and feminine and is sometimes attached to other names, e.g. Madelyn, Roslyn. In Hawaiian WAILELE is a waterfall, MEA I NOHO PILI I KA WAILELE would would be dweller by a waterfall.

The Hawaiianized-English form of LYNN = LINA, a native Hawaiian word which means soft, sticky.

LYNNETTE, LINNET is the name taken from the bird of the same name or possibly a medieval French form of the Welsh 'eiluned'—an idol. In Hawaii the linnet (California finch) was introduced quite early. It is called 'AI-MĪKANA and the name literally means papaya eater.

MABEL, MAYBELLE, and ANNABEL are from the Latin 'amabilis'—lovable. The name ANNABEL or ANNABELLE may seem closer to ANNA, however, it seems to come to from AMABEL and thus be related to MABEL. In Hawaiian lovable could be simply ALOHA. HENOHENO would be another possibility.

MAC, MACK are Celtic names which mean the son of..... (for example Mac Iver would be the son of Iver); these names are also used as diminutive forms for any name beginning with Mc or Mac. In Hawaiian OLA KA INOA means the name lives on and is said of a child bearing the name of an ancestor.

The Hawaiianized-English form of MAC and MACK is MAKA which is a native Hawaiian word that means eye or face.

MADELINE, MADELYN, and **MAGDA** are from the Greek and refer to a woman who comes from Magdela, the birthplace of the Biblical Mary Magdalene. There does not seem to be any Hawaiian equivalent for this name.

MALCOLM and COLIN are favorite Scottish names meaning a servant of St. Columba. This saint was an early Christian missionary and was also called COLIN, the dove. The Hawaiian for a dove is MANUKŪ; MANU is a bird, and KŪ imitates the cooing sound of doves. The first doves were introduced into Hawaii in 1796.

The Hawaiianized-English of COLIN is KALINA, a native Hawaiina word which means a waiting.

MAMIE. See MARY.

MANDY. See AMANDA.

MARA. See MARY.

MARCIA, MARSHA, MARCY, MARCELLA are all feminine forms of MARK.

The Hawaiianized-English of MARCIA = MALAKIA, a rarely used native Hawaiian word which means to be hurt; MARSHA = MALEKA, the Hawaiianized version of American; MARCELLA = MAKELA, the Hawaiianized version of muscles.

MARGARET is a name which has acquired many variations over time and throughout the world. A few of the more popular are: MADGE; MAGGIE; MARGE, MARGERY (the English form); MARGO, MARGOT; MARGUERITE; MARJORIE (the Scottish form); MEGAN and MEG (the Welsh form); GRETA, GRETCHEN; PEG, PEGGY. The ultimate derivation of this name which means pearl is from the Persian meaning born of moonlight. The ancient Persians believed that oysters rose from their beds at night to worship the moon, and as they reached the surface of the water they opened their shells and took in a drop of dew which was transformed by the moonbeams into a pearl. The Hawaiian word for pearl is MOMI and the phrase KU'U MOMI MAKAMAE means my precious pearl or a beloved person.

The Hawaiianized-English of MARGARET is MAKALEKA which could be a combination of the native Hawaiian words MAKA (eye or face) and LEKA (sticky, slimy).

MARIAN. MARION. French forms of MARY.

MARK, MARC are from the Roman MARCUS referring to MARS, the god of war. The feminine forms of this name are MARCIA, MARLO, MARSHA, MARCY, MARCELLA. In the ancient Hawaiian religion KŪ was the god of war, however, it would not be appropriate for a mere mortal to bear the name of such a powerful god. For the masculine forms of this name KOA meaning a warrior, and bold and fearless might be more suitable. For the feminine forms LEHUA meaning a warrior, beloved friend and also the beautiful red flowers of the 'ōhi'a tree would be suitable.

MARLIN, MARLON are Celtic forms of MERLIN. See MERVIN.

MARLO. Another form of MARK.

MARSHALL is from the Old French and refers to the official in charge of the horses, thus its meaning — a military commander. In Hawaiian 'ALIHIKAUA means a commander in battle.

MARTHA, MARTA, and **MATTY** are from the Hebrew and mean quite simply a lady. Unfortunately, the Hawaiian word for a lady—WAHINE—has been used so extensively in Hawai'i as a label for restrooms that it is no longer suitable for a given name. Perhaps LANI which means aristocratic and high born would be a better choice.

The Hawaiianized-English form of MARTHA = MALEKA which is also the Hawaiianized form of the word American; MARTA = MAKA, a native Hawaiian word which means eye; MATTIE = MALI, a native Hawaiian word which means to flatter.

MARTIN, MARTINA are, like MARK, from the name of the Roman god of war, Mars. See MARK.

MARVIN, MARV are from the Celtic and mean beautiful sea or from the Anglo-Saxon and mean sea friend. In Hawaiian KAI NANI would be beautiful sea and MAKAMAKA O KE KAI would be sea-friend.

MARY is a name which throughout time and around the world has been the most used name for girls. It has numerous variations some of which are: MARA; MARLA; MARIAM; MARIAN, MARION; MARIA, MARIE; MARIETTA; MARYLOU; MARILYN, MARLYN; MARLEEN; MAUREEN; MAMIE; MIMI; MINNIE; MITZI; MOLLY; POLLY. In spite of a great deal of research no one can be sure when or where this name was first used or what it means. Generally, it is thought to originate with the ancient Jews (in Hebrew 'mara' means bitter), but it may date back even further to ancient Egypt. In early Christian times the name MARY, since it was the name of the mother of Christ, was considered too sacred to use. During the Middle Ages it was supposed that the name was connected to the sea (Latin for sea is mar) and was interpreted as lady of the sea or star of the sea—the meaning which is generally accepted today.

In Hawaiian HŌKŪ is star and KAI is sea, so star of the sea would be HŌKŪ O KE KAI.

The Hawaiianized-English form of MARY and MARIE is MALIA, a name which is so popular that it has really become an independent name totally apart from the meaning of the native Hawaiian word MALIA - to be flattered. Other Hawaiianized-English MARY names with their Hawaiian meanings are as follows: MARA = MAKA (eye, face); MARLA = MALELA (lazy); MIMI = MIMI (to urinate); and MITZI = MIKI (quick, nimble). MAKA, MALELA, MIMI, and MIKI are all native Hawaiian words. The Hawaiianized-English of MARIA is MALAEA, a Hawaiianized form of the word Malaysia.

MATHILDA, MAUD, MATTY, TILDA, TILLY are from the Old German and mean mighty battlemaid. In ancient Hawai'i certain women were trained to fight. These women followed their husbands to battle and would rush into the conflict when they saw their husband in danger. The were called WĀHINE KOA (brave or warrior women), or WĀHINE KAUA (battle women). LEHUA, the name of the beautiful flower of the 'ōhi'a tree, was also a word applied to warriors and in addition meant beloved friend or sweetheart.

The Hawaiianized-English form of MAUD is MAKA (eye or face) and TILLY is KILI (raindrops). Both MAKA and KILI are native Hawaiian words. The Hawaiianized-English form of TILDA is KILIKA which is also the Hawaiianized form of the English word silk.

MATTHEW, the Greek form MATTHIAS, and the shortened form MATT are from the Hebrew and mean gift of the Lord. The Hawaiian equivalent for this name could be MAKANA LANI meaning heavenly gift.

MAUREEN. See MARY.

MAURICE, MORRIS are from the Latin and refer to an inhabitant of Mauretania (Morocco) thus they mean dark-complexioned. In Hawaiian 'ILI KOU means dark- skinned, or having skin the color of kou wood. Kou is a beautiful wood that the Hawaiians used to make containers, cups, and dishes.

MAXIMILIAN, MAXIM, MAX and the feminine MAXINE are from the Latin 'maximus' which means the greatest. This was a Latin title of honor given to successful military commanders. In Hawaiian MEA NUI means simply the greatest.

MAY, the name, is from the month of May which was named after MAIA, the Roman goddess of growth. It refers to the time of year when the plants began to grow after the long months of winter. NANA, according to the old Hawaiian

moon calendar, was the month of 'animation' in plants—
the beginning of the growing season.

MEGAN. A Welsh form of MARGARET.

MELANIE is from the Greek and means dark or black.
This name is connected to the story of the Greek earth goddess, MELANIA, who would go into mourning for her
daughter Spring when winter came. In Hawaiian HIWA is
a word meaning black in the sense of a desirable black-
ness. Entirely black pigs offered to the gods were called
HIWA so the word has also come to mean especially choice.
HIWAHIWA means precious, beloved and a favorite.

MELINDA and the diminutive LINDY are from the Greek
and mean the gentle. This name is sometimes associated
with LINDA, but it is actually totally different in origin and
meaning. In Hawaiian KA-MĀLIE would mean the gentle,
calm, and quiet.

MELISANDE. See MILLICENT.

MELISSA is from the Greek and means the honeybee.
In Hawaiian NALO MELI was the honeybee NALO (an
insect) plus MELI (honey).

MELODY. This name is simply the use of this musical term
as a name. In Hawaiian HONEHONE would be an appropriate equivalent. Its meaning is sweet and soft as music or a
memory of a love.

MELVIN and two feminine forms MELVINA and MELBA
are from the Anglo-Saxon and mean famous friend or chief.
In Hawaiian friend is HOALOHA and famous is KAULANA,
so famous friend would be HOALOHA KAULANA. Another
choice, which could be used for the feminine, is LEHUA. The
LEHUA are literally the beautiful red flowers of the 'ōhi'a
tree, but LEHUA is also used to mean a warrior and a
beloved friend.

MERCEDES is a Spanish name for the Blessed Virgin
meaning Maria of Mercies. In Hawaiian ALOHA means
mercy.

MEREDITH or **MERIDITH** is from the Celtic and means sea
defender. The Hawaiian equivalent would be MEA PALE O
KE KAI; MEA PALE is defender and KE KAI is the sea.

MERLE, MERYL are names which can be used in both
the masculine and feminine. They are from the French and

mean blackbird. Originally the name was applied to a person who liked to sing or whistle like a bird. In Hawaiian the 'ALALĀ is the Hawaiian crow, now found only on the Big Island. In contrast to the raucous calls of the common raven, the 'ALALĀ calls are generally mellow and musical.

The Hawaiianized-English of MERLE and MERYL is MELE which is the native Hawaiian word for a song or chant—amazingly close to the actual meaning of this name.

MERTON is an Anglo-Saxon place name meaning a town by the sea. In Hawaiian KAUHALE is the group of houses comprising a Hawaiian home and sometimes means village and KAI is sea, so for this name we would have KAUHALE MA KE KAHAKAI.

MERVIN, MERV are derived from the Welsh MERLIN—a hawk or falcon. This name may also be connected to the Celtic and mean the sea. It is related to the names MARVIN and MERWIN. In Hawaiian 'IO-LANI means the hawk of heaven and KE KAI is the sea.

MIA is a modern name which comes from the ancient Greek name Euphemia meaning of fair fame. For the Hawaiian we could have O KE KAULANA KEA.

The Hawaiian word MIA means to urinate, so it would not be appropriate to say your Hawaiian name was MIA!

MICAH is from the Hebrew and means like the Lord. MICAH was a prophet in the Bible. In Hawaiian like the Lord would be ME KA HAKU.

The Hawaiianized-English of MICAH would be MIKA which is also the Hawaiianized form of the English word Mister.

MICHAEL, the shortened forms MIKE, MICK, MICKY, and the feminine MICHELLE, MICHELE, MICHAELA, MICHAELENE, are from the Hebrew and mean 'who is God-like'. It was Michael the Archangel who led the heavenly host into a great battle against Satan and his name was the battle cry. The feminine MICHELLE may also be a flower name derived from the Michaelmas daisy. The Hawaiian for this name could be 'IHI LANI which means heavenly splendor or the sacredness of a chief. The chiefs or ali'i were believed to share the sacredness of the gods.

MILDRED, MILLIE, MILLY are Anglo-Saxon names meaning gentle power from the name of a daughter of a

7th century Anglo-Saxon king. In Hawaiian MANA is power and AKAHAI is gentle, so we would have MANA AKAHAI for this name.

The Hawaiianized-English form of MILLIE, MILLY = MILE, a native Hawaiian word for a bunch of loose olana fibers to be made into cord.

MILES, MYLES, MILO are from the Old German 'mil' and mean beloved; this could also be a place name meaning the mill. In Hawaiian there are many words for beloved including MEA ALOHA; perhaps a good choice here would be MILIA which also means beloved and is coincidentally similar to the English name.

The Hawaiianized-English of MILES, MYLES is MILEKA, the Hawaiianized form of a the Biblical grain millet. MILO = MILO, the milo tree, used by the Hawaiians in making calabashes, medicines, and dyes.

MILLICENT, MILLY the French form MELISANDE are all from the Old German and mean strong worker, energetic. In Hawaiian MIKIMIKI means quick, alert, and efficient in work.

MILTON is an English place name and means by the mill town. There would be no equivalent for this in the native Hawaiian language since mills were unknown to the ancient Hawaiians. Using the Hawaiianized-English word for mill (WILI) we would have PILI I KA HALE WILI, or MA KA HALE WILI.

MIMI is possibly a form of MARY or WILHELMINA.

MINDY is from 'Minna' which refers to the roving mime singers of the Middle Ages who committed long love songs and histories to memory. The name therefore means love memory. In Hawaiian HALI'A means sudden remembrance, especially of a loved one; and HALI'A ALOHA means cherished memory.

MINNIE. See MARY.

MIRANDA is from the Latin and means the admirable or adored one. KA-LEHIWA would be the Hawaiian equivalent with LEHIWA meaning admirable and attractive.

MITZI. See MARY.

MOLLIE, MOLLY is another form of MARY.

MONA is from the Teutonic and means the one. This name can also be a diminutive of MONICA or RAMONA. In Hawaiian the one would be KA MEA.

The Hawaiianized-English of this name would be MONA which is a variation of a native Hawaiian word, MOMONA meaning fat and fertile.

MONICA and the French form MONIQUE are of unknown origin. Several possibilities are from the Greek 'monos'—alone; from the Latin 'moneo'—I advise; or a form of DOMINICA—Sunday, a name often used for girls born on this day. For the Hawaiian KIAKAHI corresponds to the Greek alone. It means alone in the sense of the only one, unique and supreme.

The Hawaiianized-English form is MONIKA which is also the Hawaiianized form of the English word monitor.

MORGAN is a Celtic name meaning from the sea or one who lives by the sea. The Hawaiian equivalent of this name would be MAI KE KAI.

MORRIS. See MAURICE.

MURIEL is an ancient Celtic name from 'myr'-the sea and means sea-white or sea- bright. It may also be related to the Hebrew MARA—bitter. In Hawaiian the sea is KAI and white is KEA, so KAI KEA would be sea-white.

MURRAY is from the English meaning merry or from the Scottish meaning great water. In Hawaiian KAI NUI would be the great water of the ocean.

MYRA, MIRA seem to be names invented by an Elizabethan poet based on the Latin word for wonderful. In Hawaiian MEA 'Ē means wonderful and extraordinary.

The Hawaiianized-English of this name is MAILA which means then and there.

MYRNA is from the ancient Irish name Muirne meaning beloved. In Hawaiian MEA ALOHA is one way to say beloved.

MYRON is from the Greek and its possible meaning is fragrant. In Hawaiian 'A'ALA means sweet smelling and is also used to describe someone of high rank.

MYRTLE is from the Greek via the Latin and means the myrtle plant. In the language of the flowers the myrtle stands for love, so the Hawaiian of this name could be quite simply ALOHA.

123

The Hawaiianized-English form of this name is MAKALA which is also the native Hawaiian word for to loosen or untie.

NADINE, NADIA are from the Russian via the French and mean hope. In Hawaiian MANA'OLANA means hope and confidence.

NANCY, NAN, NANETTE all seem to be diminutive forms of ANN.

NAOMI is a Hebrew word meaning pleasant, beautiful, and delightful. A poetic way of saying beautiful in Hawaiian is PŪNONO which also means filled with sunshine.

NATALIE, NATALIA, NATASHA are all Russian forms of NOEL.

NATHANIEL, NATHAN and the shortened forms NAT, NATE are all from the Hebrew and mean a gift, or gift of God. The story of the prophet Nathan is in the Old Testament of the Bible. In Hawaiian, gift is MAKANA and MAKANA O KE AKUA would be gift of God.

The Hawaiianized-English form of NAT and NATE is NAKE, a native Hawaiian word for a type of fish.

NED. See EDWARD.

NELL, NELLIE. See ELEANOR.

NEIL, NIEL, NEAL, NELSON, NILES, and **NIGEL** are all related names. Their origin may be from the Celtic meaning the chief, courageous one, or champion. There is also a possible Latin meaning of dark or dark-complexioned. Both NELSON and NILES mean son of NEIL. In Hawaiian PO'OKELA is champion and KOA-LI'I means chiefly courage. ILI KOU means dark-complexioned (see Lloyd).

NICHOLAS, NICK, NICKY and the popular feminine forms NICOLA, NICOLE, NICOLETTE, NIKKI, and COLETTE are from the Greek and mean victory of the people. From St. Nick's name in Holland we get our Santa Claus. The original St. Nicholas was a 4th century bishop and is the patron saint of schoolboys and sailors. In Hawaiian LANAKILA is victory and victory of the people would be LANAKILA O KA LĀHUI.

The Hawaiianized-English of NICK is NIKA which is a modern Hawaiian word that means black (the Negro race).

NICOLE. See NICHOLAS.

124

NIGEL. Latinized form NEIL.

NILA, NYLA are invented names based on the river Nile in Egypt. There does not seem to be a Hawaiian equivalent for this name.

NINA is another form of ANN.

NOAH is a Hebrew name meaning rest and comfort. The most famous NOAH is the Biblical builder of the Ark. In Hawaiian 'OLU'OLU means cool, comfortable, and pleasant.

The Hawaiianized-English of this name would be NOA, a native Hawaiian word meaning freed of kapu.

NOEL, NOELLE, NOWELL are from the Latin 'dies natalis' meaning birthday. In French this has come to be associated primarily with the birthday of Christ— Christmas. Ever since the Middle Ages this name has been given to boys and girls born at Christmas-time. Christmas arrived in Hawai'i with the Christian missionaries and KALIKIMAKA is the Hawaiianized-English word for this festive holiday. In the ancient Hawaiian language LĀ HĀNAU was the word for birthday.

NOLAN, NOLA are from the Celtic and mean famous or noble. KAULANA is a Hawaiian word which means famous, celebrated, renowned.

NONA is Latin meaning ninth—in Roman times, when families were a bit larger, the ninth child was often given this name. In Hawaiian IWA is ninth. This should not be confused with 'IWA which is the great frigate bird and also means thief. NONA also corresponds to a native Hawaiian word which means his, hers.

NORA, NOREEN. These are shortened forms of the Latin HONORIA meaning honor. These names are very popular in Ireland. NORA may also be a shortened form of ELEANORA. In Hawaiian HANOHANO means honor and glory.

NORBERT is Germanic and means sea-bright or divinely-bright. In Hawaiian 'ALOHI LANI means the brightness of heaven, a term applied to the heavenly courts of Uli and Kapo.

NORMA is derived from the Latin and means a model or pattern. KUMU means model and pattern in Hawaiian, KUMU also means the beginning, foundation, source, teacher.

125

NORMAN is the name used in the Old English language to describe the tribes that invaded England from Normandy, therefore, the name means a northern-man. In Hawaiian KAI MAI KE 'ĀKAU means the one from the north.

OLGA is an ancient Russian name also popular in Scandanavian countries meaning holy or peace. In Hawaiian LA'A is holy and MALUHIA is the peace which surrounded religious ceremonies.

OLIVER, OLIVA, OLIVIA, OLIVE are Latin names from the olive tree, a symbol of peace. In ancient Greece the olive tree was a major source of food and fuel. Olive trees mature very slowly, therefore, if an invader destroyed the olive trees, the region was impoverished for twenty years. Only in times of lasting peace could the olive trees mature—hence the olive tree as a symbol of peace. In Hawaiian LA'IKŪ means great calm, peace, and serenity.

ORSON is from the Latin and means bear-like, therefore, strong. In Hawaiian IKAIKA is strong and powerful.

OSCAR, OSWALD and the shortened form **OZZIE** are all from the ancient Teutonic and mean divine spear or divine power. These names have been much used by Kings in Norway and Sweden. IHE LANI would be the Hawaiian equivalent of this name with IHE meaning spear and LANI heavenly and also a very high chief.

OTTO is a Germanic name meaning rich. It has long been a popular name with German and Austrian nobility. KŪ'ONO'ONO in Hawaiian means well-off and wealthy. The Hawaiianized-English of OTTO is OKO a native Hawaiian word which means to try to be better than others.

OWEN is a popular Welsh name. The meaning may be young warrior or another possible meaning from the Latin and Greek may be well-born. In Hawaiian KOA 'ŌPIO would be young warrior and MAULIAUHONUA means a descendant of chiefs of a long established line, hence well-born.

PAGE, PAIGE. In the days of chivalry this name was used for boys training to become knights. The original Greek meaning of the name is child. This name is now used for both boys and girls. The general word for child in Hawaiian is KEIKI; however, children were so beloved in ancient Hawai'i that the words LEI (a garland of flowers), PUA (a blossom) and LIKO (a newly opened leaf) were used with the meaning of a beloved child. LIKO was used especially for the child of a chief.

The Hawaiianized-English for this name is PAKE which is also the Hawaiianized form of the English word putty.

PAMELA, PAM is a made-up name. The novelist Philip Sydney in his 1580 romance, "Arcadia", called a character PAMELA. The name was created from two Greek words, 'pan'—all and 'meli'—honey. MELI is the Hawaiian word for honey and bee; therefore all honey would be MELI APAU.

PATRICK, PATRICIA, PATRICE and the shortened forms PAT, PATTY, PATSY, RICK, TRICIA, and TRISH are all derived from the word 'patrician'. Patricians were the noble class in ancient Rome, hence this name has come to mean noble birth. Since St. Patrick is the patron saint of Ireland this is a very popular Irish name. In Hawai'i the ALI'I were the noble class, LANI means high born and PUA- LANI means descendant of royalty (Lit., PUA = flower, LANI = heavenly).

The Hawaiianized-English form of PAT is PAKA, a native Hawaiian word which means to remove the dregs.

PAUL, PAULA, the French forms PAULINE, PAULETTE, and the Spanish PABLO are all derived from a Roman name meaning the small or little one. In Hawaiian KA LI'I or MEA LI'I would mean the little one. The word LI'I is also a shortened form of ALI'I which means chief.

The Hawaiianized-English form of PAULINE is POLINA, of PAULETTE it is POLEKE. These are both obsolete native Hawaiian words. The former means shiny black, the later to have lost property.

PEARL and the name PERRY which can be used for both boys and girls are jewel names first used in the late 19th century. PEARL is also sometimes used as a pet name for MARGARET since the Greek for pearl is 'margaretes'. In Hawaiian MOMI is pearl. The word MOMI is also a Ni'ihau name for a highly-prized shell used in lei making.

PEG, PEGGY are pet forms of MEG which come from MARGARET.

PENELOPE, PENNY are Greek and mean worker in cloth or one who weaves in silence. The original PENELOPE said she would remain faithful to her absent husband, Ulysses, for as long as it took her to weave a certain piece of cloth.

Each night she took out what she had woven during the day, so 20 years later, when Ulysses returned, her weaving was still unfinished. In Hawaiian MEA HANA KAPA meaning one who makes KAPA is the closest equivalent to this name. The ancient Hawaiians did not have a woven fabric, but made their clothing from the bark of the paper mulberry tree. The bark was peeled from the trees, soaked, and then pounded. The 'tapa' fabric could be very soft and fine with beautifully printed patterns. The beating of the kapa was woman's work.

PERCIVAL and **PERCY** are from the Old French. The name was invented by a 12th century poet who wrote about the quest for the Holy Grail by a hero—PERCIVAL. In the Middle Ages it became a popular name for warriors and knights. In Hawaiian the word KOA means brave and fearless and also refers to a warrior.

The Hawaiianized-English of PERCY is PELEKI, a modern word, which means brake, to apply brakes.

PERRY is a name which can be used in both the masculine and feminine. It can have several possible origins: from the French for the pear tree; from the Welsh meaning Harry's son; a diminutive of PETER; or a form of the name PEARL.

PETER, PEDRO, PIERRE, PIERCE and a feminine form PETRA are all from the Greek and mean a rock or stone. In the Bible Christ changed the name of his disciple Simon to PETER saying—"Thou art PETER and upon this rock I shall build my church." In Hawaiian PŌHAKU means rock or stone.

PHILLIP, PHILLIPA, and **PIPPA** are all from the Greek and mean a lover of horses, additional meanings are warrior and war-like. In Hawaiian KOA means brave and fearless and also a warrior.

PHOEBE is from the Greek and means the shining one. This was one of the titles given by the Greeks to the goddess of the moon. In Hawaiian KE 'ALOHI means the shining one and HINA is the ancient Hawaiian goddess of the moon.

PHYLLIS is from the Greek and means little or green leaf. A legend tells of an unfortunate princess called PHYLLIS who died for love and was changed into an almond tree. In Hawaiian LIKO means a leaf-bud and is also a term used to mean a beloved child, especially the child of a chief.

POLLY is a pet form of MARY.

PRESCOTT, PRESTON are Anglo-Saxon place names meaning respectively priest's cottage and priest's town. HALE O KE KAHUNA would mean priest's house and KAUHALE O KE KAHUNA would mean a priest's town.

PRISCILLA, PRISCA means ancient or of ancient birth in Latin. This is the name of a Roman clan and is also a Biblical name found in the Old Testament. In Hawaiian MAULIAUHONUA means descendant of old chiefs of a land, established, ancient, as a family.

PRUDENCE, PRUDY is an abstract virtue name made popular by the Puritans. In Hawaiian AKAHELE means prudent, moderate in doing anything.

QUENTIN, QUINTON, QUINCY are from the Latin and mean the fifth one. This name was often given to the fifth son in a family. In Hawaiian 'ALIMA means the fifth in a series.

QUINN is a variant of the Celtic name CONAL meaning high and mighty. In Hawaiian NU'U means high place. This word is associated with religious oracles and was also used figuratively to mean great and mighty.

The Hawaiianized-English of QUINN is KUINI, a modern Hawaiian equivalent for the English word for queen.

RACHAEL, RACHEL, RACHELLE, RAQUEL and the shortened forms RAE, RAY, SHELLY are from a Hebrew name meaning little lamb. Since the lamb was a symbol of innocence and gentleness that is what this name signifies. In Hawaiian NAHENAHE means gentle-mannered and soft-spoken; it also means sweet as music or soft as a gentle breeze.

The Hawaiianized-English form of RAE and RAY is LEI, a native Hawaiian word known around the world, meaning garland.

129

RALPH, ROLF, ROLFE are Anglo-Saxon meaning wolf counsel. In ancient times the wolf was both feared and respected for his ferocity in fighting, his intelligence, and his endurance, so this name came to mean wise counsel. In Hawaiian the saying MAKA 'OU (excelling eye) was used to describe a counselor who had served under three rulers for three generations and hence was regarded as full of wisdom.

RAMONA. Feminine of RAYMOND.

RANDOLPH, RANDALL, RANDY are Anglo-Saxon in origin meaning shield-wolf, possibly because many ancient warriors choose the wolf, who was a fierce fighter, as an emblem to emblazon on their shields. In Hawaiian KA'A KAUA refers to a person skilled in warfare, an appropriate equivalent for this name.

RAPHAEL was the name of the legendary archangel who showed Tobias how to cure his blind father, thus the name means healing of God. Its origin is from the Hebrew. In Hawaiian MAULI-OLA was the name of a god of health and means breath of life and the power of healing.

RAQUEL. See RACHAEL.

RAYMOND, RAMON, RAY and the feminine RAMONA are from an Old Germanic name made up of two words: 'ragin'—counsel, and 'mund'—protection. This was a favorite name in Europe during the Crusades. In Hawaiian MEA KIA'I means guard, preserver, and protection.

The Hawaiianized-English form of RAY is LEI, a native Hawaiian word which means a garland.

REBECCA, BECKY are from the Hebrew and originally meant a knotted cord. Just as a knotted cord should hold firm, so this name has come to be interpreted as a faithful wife. In Hawaiian PILIALO means beloved wife.

The Hawaiianized-English form of REBECCA is LEPEKA which is also the Hawaiianized form of a Biblical word for a copper coin; of BECKY it is PEKE, a a native Hawaiian word which means a dwarf or elf.

REGINA, REGAN, and the shortened form GINA are all from the Latin and mean queen. The concept of a queen was not known in ancient Hawai'i; only after the arrival of the foreigners and the establishment of a Hawaiian royalty based on European patterns were the formal titles King and Queen used. The word MŌʻĪ meant sovereign and ruler; MŌʻĪ WAHINE (female) was more specifically queen. In ancient Hawai'i the royalty were called the ALI'I and LANI was a word meaning both heavenly and a very high chief, majesty, noble, aristocratic.

The Hawaiianized-English form of GINA is KINA, which is also the Hawaiianized form of the English word meaning China.

REGINALD, REYNOLD, the Scottish RONALD along with the shortened forms REGGIE, RON and RONNIE are from the Old High German and mean power and might, thus a strong ruler or chieftain. This was another favorite warrior's name. In Hawaiian KŪPAPALANI refers to a chief of the highest rank, a strong ruler.

REGIS. See REX.

REID, REED are from the Anglo-Saxon and mean red-haired. In Hawaiian 'EHU refers to a Polynesian with a reddish tinge in the hair. These people with reddish-brown hair were considered quite a wonder among the dark-haired Polynesians.

RENÉ, RENÉE, and **RENATA** are French names from the Latin 'renatus'—reborn. In France RENÉ is the masculine and RENÉE and RENATA are the feminine. In Hawaiian HĀNAU (born) HOU (anew) would be the equivalent of this name.

REYNOLD. See REGINALD.

REX, REGIS may originally have been shortened forms of REGINALD, but they are now considered independent names from the Latin 'rex'—king. In Hawaiian MŌʻĪ means sovereign and ruler; and MŌʻĪ KĀNE (male) would be more specifically king. (see REGINA).

The Hawaiianized-English of REX is LEKA, a native Hawaiian word which means sticky, slimy.

RHODA is Greek meaning from the island of Rhodes—the island of Roses. In Hawaiian LOKE-LANI is the old-fashioned pink rose. This is also the flower emblem of the

131

island of Maui. LOKE-LANI is a relatively modern Hawaiian word since there were no roses in old Hawai'i. LOKE is the Hawaiianized form of the English word rose, and LANI means heavenly.

RHONDA and its variants RHONA and RONA are Welsh names of uncertain origin. Perhaps they come from the Lower Rhondda Valley, a great coal mining area in the south of Wales; a possible meaning is great. In Hawaiian HANOHANO is great and glorious.

The Hawaiianized-English form of RONA is LONA, a native Hawaiian word which is the block of wood used to support canoes; an additional meaning of LONA is vain, useless.

RICHARD and the shortened forms RICH, RICK, RICKY and DICK are from the German and mean strong ruler. This has always been one of the most popular boy's names; its popularity dates back to King Richard I of England—Richard the Lion-Hearted. In Hawaiian KŪPAPALANI refers to a chief of the highest rank, a strong ruler. The literal meaning is state of heavenly foundation.

The Hawaiianized-English form of RICH is LIKE, a native Hawaiian word meaning similar; RICK, RICKY = LIKI, a native Hawaiian word which means to boast or brag.

RICK. See ERIC, RICHARD.

RITA is a shortened form of MARGARITA from MARGARET. The Hawaiianized-English form is LIKA which is the Hawaiianized form of the English word liter.

ROBERT, ROBERTA, ROBIN & ROBYN, ROB, BOB, BOBBIE, BERT, and an old Germanic form RUPERT are several forms of this popular name. It is from the Anglo-Saxon and means bright fame. This name became popular in England after the Battle of Hastings in 1066 and since that time has remained one of the favorite names for boys. In Hawaiian 'IHI LANI means heavenly splendor. This was also a term used to mean the sacredness of a chief. The forms ROBIN and ROBYN are now also associated with the bird of that name.

The Hawaiianized-English form of BERT is PELEKA which is the Hawaiianized form of the English surveying term—perch.

ROCHELLE could be from the French and mean little rock. This name and its variants RACHELLE and SHELLY may also be alternate spellings of RACHEL, q.v. In Hawaiian 'ILI'ILI means a pebble or small stone. There was a hula called Hula 'ili'ili—the pebble dance.

RODERICK, a Spanish form RODRIGO, and the shortened form ROD (see also RODNEY) is an Old German combination of ROBERT and RICHARD. The resulting name means famous ruler. In Hawaiian ALI'I is ruler and KAULANA is famous and renowned, thus ALI'I KAULANA would mean famous ruler.

The Hawaiianized-English form of ROD is LOKE which is the Hawaiianized form of the word for the English flower, the rose.

RODGER and **ROGER** may be newer forms of RODNEY or as individual names they would have the meaning of famous warrior or spearman. In Hawaiian KA'A KAUA means skilled in warfare and KĀNE ME KA IHE would be spearman (KĀNE = man, IHE = spear).

RODNEY and the shorted form ROD (see also RODERICK) is an Anglo-Saxon place name meaning reed island. In Hawaiian MOKU is island and MAU'U is grassy, therefore we would have MOKU MAU'U for this name.

The Hawaiianized-English form of ROD is LOKE, which is also the Hawaiianized word for the English rose.

ROLAND—the French form; ROWLAND—the English form; and ORLANDO—the Italian form; are all names derived from the Old German meaning famous land. In the Middle Ages ROLAND was the most famous champion of the court of Charlamange. In Hawaiian 'ĀINA is land and KAULANA is famous, therefore, 'ĀINA KAULANA would be famous land.

ROLF, ROLFE. See RALPH.

RONA. See RHONDA.

RONALD. See REGINALD.

RONNIE (feminine) is a shortened form of VERONICA; (masculine) is a shortened form of RONALD.

RORY is a Celtic name meaning ruddy, and red-haired. Three high kings of Ireland were named RORY. In Hawaiian 'EHU refers to Polynesians with a red tint to their hair. These 'EHU were considered quite a wonder in old Hawai'i and it is an anthropological mystery how these 'red-heads' became a part of the dark-haired Polynesian race.

The Hawaiianized-English form of RORY is LOLI, a native Hawaiian word meaning to change or alter.

ROSE, ROSA and its many variants some of which are: ROASLIE; ROSALEEN; ROSITA; ROSALYN and ROSALIND (pretty rose); ROSAMUND (rose of the world) are names that have ancient origins. In the earliest Germanic form—'hros' actually meant 'horse'. However, this meaning from the remote past has now been totally replaced by the Latin flower name—rose. The Hawaiian name would be LOKE-LANI. LOKE is the Hawaiianized-English word for the English rose and LANI means heavenly and royal.

ROSEMARY can be a combination name of ROSE and MARY; or the name of the plant ROSEMARY which derives its name from the Latin meaning dew of the sea; in the language of the flowers ROSEMARY signifies remembrance. KĒHAU O KE KAI would be dew of the sea and HALI'A means sudden remembrance, especially of a loved one.

ROSS has many possible origins and meanings, you can take your pick! As a Scottish and Gāelic place name it means headland; from the Old French it could mean red; from the Anglo-Saxon—horse; or it may be a masculine form of ROSE. In Hawaiian LAE means promontory or headland. This is also the word for forehead and by extension a word for wisdom.

The Hawaiianized-English form is LOKO, a native Hawaiian word which means inside, interior.

ROWENA is from the Celtic and means slender and fair. In the novel 'Ivanhoe' ROWENA is the heroine. In ancient Hawai'i the word KIOEA or KIOWEA was used to describe a slender person. This is also the name for a migratory shore bird that visits Hawai'i in the winter months. The name of this long-legged bird came to be associated with long-legged, slender persons. MĀ'ILA means light skin and also clear as the sea on a sunny day. If you wish to combine these two words you would have MEA KIOEA A ME MĀ'ILA.

ROXANN, ROXANNE is Persian place name meaning the brilliant or the arising dawn. In Hawaiian KA WENA is the glow of sunrise and HUAKA means dazzling and clear as crystal.

ROY and a possible feminine form ROYAL can have two origins and meanings—the original is probably Celtic meaning red-haired; however, since the French word for king is 'roi' it may also have this meaning. In old Hawai'i 'EHU was the word used to describe Polynesians with a red tinge to their hair. The 'EHU were quite a wonder and it is an anthopological mystery how these 'red-heads' appeared among the dark-haired Polynesians. In ancient Hawaiian society the royalty were the ALI'I and LANI means a very high chief, royal and high born. In more modern times the kings and queens of Hawai'i had the title MŌ'Ī.

The Hawaiianized-English form of ROY is LOI, a native Hawaiian word which means to look over critically.

ROYDEN is an English name via the Latin and means from the king's valley. The Hawaiian form of this name would MAI KE AWĀWA O KE ALI'I.

RUBY is from a Latin word for red and is a jewel name referring to this precious red stone. In Hawaiian HI'OHI'O means bright red. The Hawaiians did not have a word for ruby, however the word HI'OHI'O was seldom used, so this rare word seems appropriate for this rare jewel.

The Hawaiianized-English form of RUBY is LUPE, a native Hawaiian word for a kite.

RUPERT. Old Germanic form of ROBERT.

RUDOLF, RUDOLPH, RUDY are all from the Germanic and mean famous wolf, no doubt a reference to a renowned warrior. This was a name much favored among Austrian nobility. In Hawaiian KOA KAULANA would mean renowned warrior; KOA is brave and also warrior, and KAULANA is famous and renowned.

The Hawaiianized-English form of RUDY is LUKE which is the Hawaiianized form of RUDY IS LUKE which is the Hawaiianized form of the English lute.

RUSSELL, RUSS, RUSTY is from the Old French and means red-haired. In medieval England the red fox was known as a RUSSELL. 'EHU refers to Polynesians with a reddish tinge to their hair. Among the dark-haired Polynesians the 'EHU were considered quite a wonder and anthropologists have yet to discover how these 'red-heads' came to be a part of the Polynesian race.

RUTH is a Hebrew name meaning vision of beauty or friend. There is a Book of Ruth in the Old Testament of the Bible. At one time the name RUTH meant pity or sorrow and was given as a virtue name like Faith and Hope. In Hawaiian HIHI'O O KA NANI would be vision of beauty and a friend is HOALOHA.

The Hawaiianized-English of RUTH is LUKA which is also the Hawaiianized form of the English surveying term rood.

RYAN is from the Gāelic and means little king. The Hawaiian LI'I is an interesting equivalent for this name. LI'I means small and little and is also short for ALI'I which means chief or king.

RYDER, RIDER is from the Old English and means a knight or horseman. Since the Hawaiians did not have horses the name that would come closest to this name would be one of the warrior names such as AU KANAI'I which literally means a strong current of the ocean, therefore, a warrior of exceptional strength.

SACHA. See ALEXANDER.

SADIE. See SARAH.

SALLY. See SARAH.

SALOME, SOLOMON, and **SELIMA** are all from a Hebrew word meaning peaceful. The most famous people to have this name were both Biblical, SOLOMON in the Old Testament and SALOME in the New. SALOME, however, was anything but peaceful since she demanded the head of John the Baptist on a platter! In Hawaiian MALUHIA means peace, quiet, and serenity.

SAMUEL, SAM and the feminine SAMUELA, SAMANTHA are all from the Hebrew. The name means God has heard. The Biblical SAMUEL was so wise his name came to be a synonym for a judge. In Hawaiian God has heard would be UA LOHE KE AKUA.

SANDRA, SANDY, SONDRA. See ALEXANDER and CASSANDRA.

SARA, SARAH and the variants SADIE, SALLY, SARI, and SHARI (a Hungarian form) are all from the Hebrew. In the Bible Abraham's wife was first called 'Sarai'- the quarrelsome, but by divine decree this was changed to SARAH, and with the change of one letter it became the princess. In

Hawaiian KAMĀLI'I means royal child and KAMĀLI'I WAHINE would be a princess.

Following are the Hawaiianized-English forms of the SARA names which correspond to native Hawaiian words: SARA, SARAH = KALA, to loosen and also the surgeon-fish; SALLY = KALE, watery; SADIE = KAKI, cross, irritable; SARI = KALI, to wait.

SCOT, SCOTT. This name quite naturally means a person from Scotland. The first inhabitants of what is now Scotland were roving Irish tribes so the name could also mean wanderer. In Hawaiian KI'IHELE means a gadabout and wanderer; and 'IMI LOA means a distant traveller.

The Hawaiianized-English form of SCOTT is KOKA which is also the Hawaiianized form of the English word soda.

SEAN. See JOHN.

SELINA, SELENA, SELENE, CELINA, CELINE, CELINDA and **CENA** are from the Greek name for Artemis, the goddess of the moon. In ancient Hawai'i HINA was the goddess of the moon and MAHINA means the moon.

The Hawaiianized-English form of CENA is KENA, a native Hawaiian word which means quenched or satisfied as of thirst.

SELMA is a Celtic name meaning the fair one. This is most likely a feminine form of Anselm. KA MEA LAMALAMA means the fair-complexioned one, LAMALAMA also means bright-looking, animated and vivacious .

SERENA is from the Latin and means the calm and serene. In Hawaiian MĀLIE means calm and quiet.

SETH is from the Hebrew and means the appointed or chosen. In the Bible SETH was the son of Adam and Eve following Cain and Abel. In Hawaiian KA MEA HO'O-KOHO'IA would mean the chosen one.

The Hawaiianized-English of SETH is KEKA which is also the Hawaiianized- English word for sex or gender.

SHANE. From SEAN, an Irish form of JOHN.

SHANNON. This name is now used for both boys and girls. It is from the Celtic and means slow waters and it is also a place name from the River Shannon in Ireland. In Hawaiian NĀ WAI LOHI would be slow waters.

SHANTEL. See CHANTAL.

SHARI. A variant of CHARLES, SARAH, or SHARON.

SHARLENE. A modern variant of CHARLENE, which is in turn derived from CHARLES.

SHARON, SHARI. In Palestine there is an area called SHARON meaning level plain. This area is famous for its fertility and there is a variety of hibiscus that grows there called the Rose of SHARON. From this flower comes this name. In Hawaiian ALOALO is the native white hibiscus. Since 1923 the hibiscus has been the flower of Hawai'i.

The Hawaiianized-English of this name is KĀLONA a Hawaiian word which also means an old horse or slowpoke.

SHAUN, SHAUNA, SHAWN. See JOHN.

SHEBA is a Biblical place name for an area of southwest Arabia or a shortening of Bathsheba which means daughter of our oath. The rather lengthy Hawaiian equivalent of this name would be KAIKAMAHINE (daughter) KŌ MĀUA HO'OHIKI (oath).

The Hawaiianized-English form is KEPA, a native Hawaiian word which means notched.

SHEILA, SHEILAH. These are possibly Old Irish forms of CECELIA or possibly quite another Hebrew name meaning the asked for or wanted one. In Hawaiian MAKAKĒHAU means the heart's desire, and 'ANO'I means the wanted one.

The Hawaiianized-English of this name is KILA, a native Hawaiian word which means a high place.

SHELBY is from the Teutonic and is a form of SELBY meaning from the manor farm. Recently this name, which was originally masculine, has also been used for girls. In Hawaiian MAI KA MAHI means from the farm.

SHELDON, SHELTON and possibly a masculine SHELLY are derived from an English place name meaning hut on a hill or shell island. For the Hawaiian MOKU PŪPŪ would be shell island. The famous leis of Ni'ihau made with beautiful small shells are lei pūpū.

SHELLEY. See ROCHELLE, MICHELLE (MICHAEL), and SHIRLEY.

SHERRY, SHERI (which may also be a phonetic variant of CHÉRIE), and possibly SHERLE could be names based on the Spanish wine, sherry, which is named for the village of Xeres where it is made. More likely these names are derived from the French 'chérie' meaning cherished one. In Hawaiian NĒNĒ HIWA means beloved, precious, and cherished one.

SHIRLEY, SHIRL, SHELLEY, and **SHERYL** are based on an English place name. SHIRELY began as a boy's name and only after 1850 did it have a sex-change to a name now used almost exclusively for girls. The meaning is from the shire meadow. In Hawaiian MAI KE KULA means from the meadow.

SIBYL, SYBIL. In ancient Greece a sybil was a woman who claimed to be able to interpret the wishes of the gods through oracles. Thus, the name has come to mean a prophetess. In Hawaiian MEA MAKA 'IKE means one who sees clearly and with keen powers of observation; to see more than most, especially supernatural things.

SIDNEY, SYDNEY. This was originally a family name and referred to someone who came to England from St. Denis, France. The name is a contraction of 'saint' and 'Denis' meaning from St. Denis. We can find no Hawaiian equivalent for this name.

SIGRID is a popular Scandanavian name meaning beautiful victory or favorite. In Hawaiian PUNAHELE means a favorite.

SIMON, SIMEON and a feminine form SIMONE are either from the Hebrew meaning the hearing or from the Greek meaning snub-nosed. In Hawaiian KOKI is snub-nosed, if you don't want your Hawaiian name to be snub-nosed KŌKĪ means topmost and NANI KŌKĪ means supremely beautiful!

SIOBHAN. Irish form of JOAN which is in turn derived from JOHN.

SOLOMON. See SALOME.

SONIA, SONYA. See SOPHIA.

SOPHIA and the Russian variants SONIA, SONYA are derived from the Greek word for wisdom. In Hawaiian MAHAO'O means someone mature in wisdom; MANA'O AKAMAI means spirit of wisdom.

STACEY, STACY are shortened forms of ANASTASIA or EUSTACIA. This name has now become so popular that it has established itself as an independent name. Its meaning, however, would come from the Greek of the original names and be resurrection or steadfast. In Hawaiian 'ONIPA'A means firm and steadfast. This was the motto of Ka-mehameha V and Lili'u-o-ka-lani.

STANLEY and its shortened form STAN are old English place names and mean from the stone field or stony meadow. In Hawaiian KULA is meadow and 'ILI-'ILI is a pebble or small stone, so KULA 'ILI-'ILI would be a stony meadow.

STELLA, and the variant ESTELLE are from the Latin and mean star. The Hawaiian word for star is HŌKŪ.

The Hawaiianized-English is KELE, a native Hawaiian word which means watery, swampy.

STEPHEN, STEPHAN, STEVEN, STEVE and the feminine forms STEPHANIE and STEFFIE are derived from the Greek 'stephanas' meaning a crown or wreath. This referred to the wreath of laurel leaves awarded to athletic champions. In Hawaiian a LEI is a wreath or garland. In ancient Hawai'i, just as in ancient Greece, leis were given to the winners of athletic contests. A winner of an athletic contest would be called PO'OKELA which means champion or foremost.

STEWART, STUART are names derived from a Scottish royal family name. Originally the name came from 'sty-ward'—a person who looked after animals (not necessarily pigs) intended for meat. Thus the name acquired the meaning caretaker and guardian. In Hawaiian MEA KIA'I means guard, caretaker, and preserver.

SUSAN, SUSANNA, SUZANNE, SUZETTE, SUSIE, SUZY are all derived from the Bible. In the Old Testament there is a Persian city called 'shushannah'—the city of the white lilies. The meaning of this name is therefore a lily; SUZETTE is a little lily. 'UKI'UKI is the general Hawaiian name for native Hawaiian members of the lily family found mostly in the forest around Kī-lau-ea Volcano. However, since UKIUKI without the stops (') is the Hawaiian word for anger perhaps a better choice for the SUSAN names would be PA'INIU, another species of Hawaiian lily. In olden days Hawaiians made hat leis of PA'INIU to show that they had visited Pele at Kī-lau-ea.

The Hawaiianized-English form of SUSIE and SUZY is KUKE, a native Hawaiian word which means to nudge or push.

SYLVIA, SILVIA, SILVIE and the less popular masculine forms SYLVESTER and SILAS are from the Latin 'silva'—woods, therefore the name means a dweller in the woods or forest. In Hawaiian MAKANAHELE means wild, untamed, of the wilderness, literally a forest-person.

TAB is a shortened form of several last names such as Taber, Talbot. It is now sometimes used as a first name. These names are all derived from the French 'tambour' meaning drummer. It is also possible that TAB is an invented first name just like the name of a diet soda, and has no real meaning! In Hawaiian MEA HO'OKANI PAHU means the person who sounds the drums (PAHU).

The Hawaiianized-English form of TAB is KAPA which is also the tapa cloth made by the Hawaiians from the bark of the paper mulberry tree.

TAD, THAD. See THADDEUS, and THEODORE.

TAMARA, TAMA, and the form TAMMY which can also be a feminine form of THOMAS, are from the Hebrew and mean the palm tree. The palm tree was a symbol of beauty and fruitfulness hence the name has come to mean graceful and upright. In ancient Hawai'i the coconut palm was as important as the palms found in Biblical lands. The coconut palm, called NIU, provided food, cordage, thatch, drums, and many other things. This name could therefore be NIU or possibly NIOLO which means upright and stately.

The Hawaiianized-English form of TAMARA is KAMALA which could be a combination of KA (the) and a native Hawaiian word MALA that means both aching and sour; TAMA = KAMA which is a native Hawaiian word for a child.

TAMMY. See TAMARA and THOMAS.

TANIA, TANYA are possibly abbreviations of the Russian TATIANA or a form of the Anglo-Saxon TATE which means cheerful. In Hawaiian HAU'OLI MAU mean always happy, cheerful.

TATE. See TANIA.

TED, TEDDY. See EDWARD and THEODORE.

TERENCE, TERRENCE, TORRANCE, TORIN and the diminutive TERRY are from the Latin and mean smooth and tender. There is also an additional Irish meaning—the towering. In Hawaiian HALEHALE means high and towering as a cliff or the waves.

141

TERESA, THERESA, THERESE and the diminutives TESS, TESSIE, TRACY, TERRY are of uncertain origin, possibly the meaning is from the Greek, a reaper or farmer. This name seems to have first been used in Spain in the 6th century. In Hawaiian MAHI 'AI means a farmer and with the first letter capitalized it is also the name of a star.

The Hawaiianized-English of TESS is KEKA which is also the Hawaiianized- English word for sex or gender.

TESS. See TERESA and ELIZABETH.

THADDEUS and the short forms TAD, THAD are the Greek and Latin forms of the name JUDAS meaning praise or praise God. In Hawaiian MILILANI means to praise and exalt.

The Hawaiianized-English form of TAD and THAD is KAKI, a native Hawaiian word which means cross and irritable.

THANE is from the Anglo-Saxon and means an attendant of the king. The word KA'ALANI means a member of the royal court, hence an attendant of the king.

The Hawaiianized-English form of this name is KĀNE which means man. When capitalized it is also the name of the leading god in the ancient religion—the god of creation and sunlight to whom no human sacrifices were made. It is perhaps a bit presumptuous for a mere mortal to take the name of the great god KĀNE.

THELMA is a modern name invented for the 1887 novel "Thelma—a Norwegian Princess"—its meaning seems to be from the Greek—infant or youth. In Hawaiian PŪNUA means a young bird or fledgling and has also come to be used as a word for a young child or sweetheart.

The Hawaiianized-English form of THELMA is KELAMA which is the Hawaiianized form of dram, the English unit of measure.

THEODORE and its shortened forms TED, TEDDY, THEO and the feminine form THEODORA with its shortened forms DORA, DORI, and THEA are from the Greek and mean gift of God. In Hawaiian MAKANA LANI would mean heavenly gift and MAKANA O KE AKUA would be gift of God.

The Hawaiianized-English forms of this name which correspond to native Hawaiian words are: DORA = KOLA which means hard, sexually excited; DORI = KOLI, to whittle or sharpen. TED is KEKA a Hawaiianized form of the English word for sex, gender.

142

THERESA, THERESE. See TERESA.

THOMAS, the short forms TOM, TOMMY; the feminine form THOMASINA and its shortened form TAMMY are all from the Hebrew and mean twin. St. Thomas the apostle was supposed to be a twin and the first bearer of this name. In Hawaiian twin is MĀHOE or MĀHANA.

The Hawaiianized-English of THOMAS, TOM, TOMMY is KOMA which is also the Hawaiianized-English word for the comma; TAMMY = KAMA, a native Hawaiian word for a child.

THOR is an Old Norse name meaning thunder. THOR was the chief Norse god and the sound of his hammer made thunder. In Hawaiian thunder is HEKILI.

The Hawaiianized-English of this name is KOLA which means hard, sexually excited.

TIARE is a flower name, the fragrant Tahitian gardenia. NĀNŪ is the name for several native Hawaiian species of gardenias.

TIFFANY. This name was originally a shortened form of the Greek 'epiphanius' meaning 'of the manifestation', but its popularity today is from its association with New York's classy Fifth Ave. jewelry store of the same name. In keeping with the modern associations of this name we have chosen for the Hawaiian LINOHAU which means beautifully decorated, ornamented—which certainly describes Tiffany's wares.

TILDA, TILLY. See MATHILDA.

TIMOTHY and the shortened form TIM are from the Greek and mean to honor or fear God. In Hawaiian ILIHIA means stricken with awe and reverence; thrilled as by beauty.

TINA is an ending of several names such as CHRISTINA, BETTINA or as an independent name it would mean the little or small one. In Hawaiian MEA LI'I would be the little one.

The Hawaiianized-English form of TINA is KINA which is also the Hawaiianized form of the English word for China, Chinese.

TISH. See LETITIA.

TOBEY, TOBY is possibly from the Hebrew TOBIAS meaning God is just, or a Germanic name meaning a dove. TOBY is a popular Irish form. KŪPONO KE AKUA means GOD (AKUA) is just (KŪPONO); and MANU KŪ is the name the Hawaiians invented for the introduced dove. MANU is bird and KŪ sounds like the cooing sound made by doves.

TODD has several possible origins and meanings. From the Scottish and Norse it would mean a fox; from the Old English a thicket. Since there were no foxes in old Hawaiian we will use the Old English for the Hawaiian equivalent. NĀHELEHELE means a forest or thicket in Hawaiian.

The Hawaiianized-English of this name is KOKA which is the Hawaiianized form of the English word soda.

TONI, TONY. See ANTHONY.

TORIN, TORRANCE. See TERENCE.

TRACEY, TRACY could be from the Old French and mean a road or path; from the Old English it would mean brave. This name is currently used for both boys and girls. TRACY is also a possible variant of TERESA. In Hawaiian ALANUI means a large path or road. A poetic name for the equator was alanui a ke ku'uku'u— the road of the spider. In Hawaiian KOA is a word used to mean brave.

TRAVERS, TRAVIS is from the Old French and means from the crossroad. In Hawaiian MAI KA HUINA ALANUI means from the crossing-path.

The Hawaiianized-English form of this name is KAWELO, the name of a mythological hero about whom there are many old Hawaiian legends.

TREVOR is from the Celtic and means the prudent. In Hawaiian AKAHELE means cautious and prudent.

TRICIA, TRISH. See PATRICIA.

TRINA. From KATRINA, see KATHERINE.

TRIXIE. See BEATRICE.

TROY is from the Old French and means at the place of the curly-haired people. In Hawaiian KĀPI'I refers to a person with curly hair. These curly-haired persons were believed to be strong, hence good warriors.

The Hawaiianized-English of TROY is KOI, a native Hawaiian word meaning to urge or implore.

TRUDIE, TRUDY. See GERTURDE.

TYRONE is from the Greek and means lord or ruler. This name is probably related to the word 'tyrant'. In Hawaiian HAKU was a term meaning lord or master and used when addressing a chief.

UNA is a Gāelic and English name from the Latin word for one. In Hawaiian KA MEA is the one. UNA is also a native Hawaiian word which means the shell of the turtle.

UPTON is an Anglo-Saxon place name meaning from the hill town. In Hawaiian NOHO UKA is an upland dweller.

URANIA is from the Greek and means heavenly. In mythology URANIA was the Muse of astronomy. In Hawaiian LANI means heavenly.

URSULA is from the Latin and means little she-bear. The Latin word for bear is 'ursus'. There were no bears in old Hawai'i so we will go back to a Greek myth for the Hawaiian equivalent for this name. There is a Greek myth of a maiden transformed by Zeus, the king of the gods, into a bear and placed in the heavens. The maiden became the constellation we call the 'Little Dipper'—the correct name for this constellation is 'Ursa Minor' or the 'Little Bear' and the most important star in 'Ursa Minor' is the North Star, known to the Hawaiians as KIO-PA'A. Thus we come to KIO-PA'A as a Hawaiian equivalent for this name.

VALENTINE, VALENTINA is from the Latin meaning healthy and strong. February 14, the day on which St. Valentine became a martyr, coincided with an ancient pagan festival on which lots were drawn for lovers, thus our association of Valentine's Day with lovers. In Hawaiian KILAKILA means majestic and strong.

VALERIE, VALERYE is from the Latin and means strong. The similar name VALERIA is actually from the ancient herb valerian or catnip which was sacred in cat- worshipping ancient Egypt. In Hawaiian KILAKILA means majestic, strong, and having poise that commands admiration.

VANCE and the diminutive VAN are from the Dutch and mean Van's son or an English occupation name meaning a thresher. In Hawaiian OLA KA INOA means the name lives on and is used when a family name is given to a child.

VANESSA could be a form of the Greek word for the goddess Phanessa which is derived in turn from the Greek word for butterfly. In Hawaiian PULELEUHA means butterfly. There is a native Hawaiian butterfly called 'Vanessa tameamea'—the Ka-mehameha butterfly.

VAUGHN is from the Welsh and means small. In Hawaiian LI'I means small and is also an abbreviated form of ALI'I meaning royal or kingly.

VELMA. See WILLIAM.

VERA is used in Russia to mean faith, it is derived from the Latin for true. A related name is VERITY which means truth. In Hawaiian 'OIA'I'O means truth and faithfulness.

VERNON and the feminine variations VERNA and LAVERNE are from the Latin and French and mean to grow green or to flourish. This name is connected with the spring season and was frequently given to children born in the spring. In Hawaiian LUPALUPA means flourishing, of luxuriant growth, lush; KUPULAU refers to the spring season (literally, it means leaf sprouting).

VERONICA frequently shortened to RONNIE, is from the Greek and means true image. The name is from the legend about a young maiden who handed Christ a handkerchief on his way to Calvary. After he had wiped his face with the cloth his image was miraculously imprinted on it. In Hawaiian KE AO means the exact image. AO is a word of many meanings in Hawaiian, the primary of which is daylight.

VICTOR, the diminutive VIC and the feminine VICTORIA and VICKY are from the Latin and mean, as you might expect, victory. In Hawaiian LANAKILA is victory.

The Hawaiianized-English form of VICTORIA is WIKOLIA which is the Hawaiianized form of an English word for a fine lawn fabric used in dresses.

VINCENT and the diminutives VINCE and VINNIE are from the Latin 'vincere' meaning to conquer. In Hawaiian NA'I means both to conquer and conqueror. One title for Ka-mehameha was—O Ka-mehameha ka na'i aupuni—Ka-mehameha, conqueror of the nation.

VIOLA, VIOLET and a French form YOLANDE are from an Italian flower name for the woodland violet. The name has come to mean modest because of the shy habits of this woodland flower. NANI WAI'ALE'ALE is the name for a native Hawaiian violet found only in high bogs on the islands of O'ahu and Kaua'i, the literal meaning is Wai'ale'ale beauty. In Hawaiian AKAHAI means modest, shy, thoughtful, and kind.

146

VIRGINIA and the diminutive GINNY are the feminine forms of the seldom used masculine VIRGIL. From the Latin, this name means a twig, or unbloomed—hence a virgin. The state of Virginia was named by Sir Walter Raleigh after Queen Elizabeth, known as The Virgin Queen. In Hawaiian PŪLOKU means comely, tender as a virgin. It also has another meaning—bright and sparking as sunshine.

The Hawaiianized-English of GINNY is KINI, a native Hawaiian word which means a multitude.

VIVIAN, VIVIEN and the variant VITA are from the Latin and mean life, hence vital and animated. This name was used for both boys and girls with VIVIAN being the feminine form and VIVIEN the masculine. In Hawaiian LAMALAMA means bright, animated, vivacious; an additional meaning is fair-complexioned.

WADE is from the Teutonic and means one who 'wades' or wanders, therefore a wanderer. In Teutonic legends a 'wade' was thought of as a demon of the sea or of storms. In Hawaiian LAU HALA LANA is a saying used for a wanderer, the literal meaning is a lauhala leaf floating on the sea.

WALDO is from the Old High German and means to wield, referring to the strength and power of a ruler. In Hawaiian MĀHUAHUA denotes strength, especially the strength and power of a ruler.

WALLACE, WALLIS and the shortened form WALLY are all from what was originally a Scottish family name. In England this name came to mean a foreigner or stranger, especially a Welshman. The form WALLIS was at one time used for both boys and girls. In Hawaiian MEA 'Ē is a word that means extraordinary, unusual, wonderful and also is used to mean a stranger or a person of another race.

The Hawaiianized-English form of WALLY is WALI, a native Hawaiian word which means smooth or thin (as thin poi).

WALTER and the shortened form WALT are from the German and mean powerful warrior or ruling the people. KOA KONAPILIAHI means strong and powerful (KONAPILIAHI) warrior (KOA).

WANDA is from the Teutonic 'Wendla'. This word is of uncertain meaning but it most likely is related to 'wanderer'. In Hawaiian 'IMI LOA means a distant traveller, a seeker and hence also some with deep knowledge. (see also WADE)

147

WARD is from the Old English and means a warder or watchman. In Hawaiian KŪ UAKI is a watchman, a sentinel, and a guardian.

WARREN and the related names WARNER and WERNER are modern English variants of the original German 'varin', probably meaning defender. In Hawaiian MEA KIA'I means preserver and KA MEA KIA'I I NA KANAKA means preserver or defender of men (i.e. mankind).

WARRICK is from the Teutonic and means war king; another origin may be from the Welsh meaning guardian of the bay. This was a popular English nobility name used by dukes and earls. For king we could use the more ancient word ALI'I meaning chief, or the more modern MŌ'Ī from the days of the monarchy meaning king. The word for war is KAUA, so we would have ALI'I KAUA or MŌ'Ī KAUA.

WAVERLEY is from the Teutonic and means the rippling lea (a lea is a grassland or pasture). In Hawaiian KULA is a meadow or grassland and 'ALE is rippling, so we would have the combination KULA 'ALE 'ALE.

WAYNE is an English version of the Teutonic WAIN-WRIGHT meaning a maker of wagons. Originally a last name, the fame of Anthony Wayne, a Revolutionary War hero, helped to popularize this as a first name. There does not seem to be a Hawaiian equivalent for this name.

WENDELL in Teutonic means a wanderer. Literally, it means a Slav. In the Middle Ages the Slavs were known as the Wends or wanderers. The Hawaiian equivalent of this name could be 'IMI LOA, the same translation we have chosen for the related feminine WANDA.

WENDY is a name that the author of "Peter Pan", James Barry, claims he invented from baby talk syllables! It is also possible that the name is a shortened form of WENDELL thus meaning a wanderer. It is also considered a shortened form of GWENDOLYN or GENEVIEVE. See these various names for Hawaiian equivalent meanings.

WESLEY, the variant WESTLY, and the shortened forms WES and WEST are all from an English place name meaning west field or meadow. Originally a last name, it became popular as a first name when used to honor the founder of the Methodist religion, John Wesley. The Hawaiian equiva-

lent would be KULA (meaning a meadow) and KOMO-
HANA (the west, referring to the sun 'entering' the sea in the
west); so we would have the combined KULA KOMOHANA.

WHITNEY is from the Anglo-Saxon and means from the
white place. There are a host of related names some of
which are: WHITBY, WHITLAW, WHITFIELD, WHITFORD,
WHITLEY, and WHITLOCK. In Hawaiian KŪLANA is place
and KEA is white so we would have MAI KE KŪLANA KEA
for from the white place.

WILBUR, WILBERT see GILBERT.

WILFRED, WILFRID is a combination of two Anglo-Saxon
words, will and peace, so the name signifies a peacemak-
er. In Hawaiian KA I HO'OMALU means one who makes
peace.

WILHELMINA, WILLA and **WILMA** are feminine forms of
the German WILHELM, a form of WILLIAM.

WILLIAM and its numerous shortened forms BILL, BILLY,
WILL, WILLY; LIAM (an Irish form), and the feminine forms
WILLA, WILMA, WILHELMINA, VELMA are all from the Old
High German words meaning 'will' and 'helmet' and can
be seen in the German form of this name WILHELM. The
meaning is a powerful warrior or protector. For many years
WILLIAM was second only to John as the most popular first
name for boys. For the masculine forms of this name we
would choose the Hawaiian AU KANAI'I meaning a strong
warrior, literally a strong current. For the feminine forms
LEHUA. The LEHUA are the beautiful red flowers of the 'ōhi'a
tree. Additional meanings for LEHUA are warrior, beloved
friend, and sweetheart.

WINFRED the feminine WINIFRED, and the shortened
form WINNIE are Anglo-Saxon forms of the Welsh name
Gwenfrew meaning blessed reconciliation. The English,
unable to pronounce the Welsh, changed the name to the
nearest sounding Anglo- Saxon name meaning a friend of
peace. In Hawaiian friend is HOALOHA and peace is MALU
so we would have HOALOHA O KA MALU for friend of
peace.

WINONA is an American Indian name meaning first
born daughter. It was popularized by the the American poet
William Wadsworth Longfellow in the poem "Hiawatha". In

Hawaiian a daughter is KAIKAMAHINE and HIAPO means a first-born child, so the Hawaiian equivalent would be KAIKAMAHINE HIAPO.

WINSTON is an Anglo-Saxon place name from a town in Gloucestershire probably meaning 'Wine's settlement' with the meaning of 'wine' being 'friend'. In Hawaiian 'AIKAPA means a privileged friend, generally one who shares in the profits of a friend's land.

WOODROW is an Anglo-Saxon place name meaning passage in the woods. ALA (road, path) plus NAHALE (woods) would give us ALA NAHALE for this name.

WRIGHT is an Anglo-Saxon occupation name meaning worker or artisan. In Hawaiian NO'EAU means clever, skillful, artistic; and HANA LIMA 'IKE means an expert craftsman.

WYATT is a relatively modern English version of the Old French GUY.

WYMAN is from the Anglo-Saxon and means a wayman or foot soldier. In ancient Hawai'i the word KOA was used to refer to a citizen-soldier. KOA also is the name of a magnificent Hawaiian forest tree and has the additional meaning of brave.

WYNN is from the Anglo-Saxon and means white. WYNNE may be a variant of this or an independent name meaning champion. In Hawaiian KEA is white, and PO'OKELA means foremost, champion.

XAVIER and the feminine XAVIERA are from the Arabic and mean the bright and the splendid. This name was introduced into Spain during the Moorish occupation. The name is often given in memory of the Spanish nobleman and saint, Francis Xavier. In Hawaiian KE 'ALOHI LANI means heaveanly splendor, the brightness of heaven.

YVES and the feminine forms YVONNE and YVETTE are French variants of the Old Scandanavian IVER, an archer. In Hawaiian the word for an archer is PANA PUA. PANA means to shoot and PUA is the Hawaiian word for a flower. PUA came also to mean an arrow because arrows were sometimes made from the flower stalks of the sugar cane plant.

ZACHARY, ZACHERY and the shortened form ZACK are the traditional English versions of the Hebrew ZACHARIAH meaning memory of the Lord. In the Old Testament this name is used for a priest, a prophet, and a King of Israel. In Hawaiian HALI'A means a sudden remembrance, especially of a loved one, and HALI'A O KA HAKU would be memory of the Lord.

ZARED is from the Hebrew and means the luxuriant. In Hawaiian OHO LUPALUPA means abundant and luxuriant, as plants or hair tresses.

ZEBADIAH, ZEBEDEE are from the Hebrew and mean the Lord has remembered. UA HO'OMANA'O KA HAKU would be the Hawaiian equivalent, HO'OMANA'O is to remember.

ZELDA is a diminutive of the Teutonic GRISELA signifying gray battle-maid or grey heroine. In ancient Hawai'i certain women were taught to fight and followed their husbands into battle. These women would rush into the conflict when they saw their husband in danger, or even take the place of a husband who was killed in battle. They were called KOA WĀHINE (brave women) or WĀHINE KAUA (battle women). If we add 'ĀHINAHINA which means gray to this we would have KOA WAHINE 'ĀHINAHINA for gray battle-maid, or ME'E 'ĀHINAHINA for grey heroine.

ZERLINDE is from the Hebrew via Latin and means beautiful dawn. In Hawaiian AO is the dawn and NANI is beautiful, so we would have AO NANI for this unusual name.

ZITA is from the Hebrew and means mistress. In times past 'mistress' was a title of respect used in the same way as 'Lady'. St. Zita became the patroness of Italy. In Hawaiian WAHINE is a woman or lady, however, this word has been used so much as a label for restrooms that LANI, with its meaning of aristocratic would be more appropriate.

The Hawaiianized-English form of ZITA is KIKA, a native Hawaiian word which means slippery, slimy with mud.

ZOE is a Greek rendering of EVE meaning life. It was pronounced to rhyme with joy but is now usually ZO-ee. In Hawaiian OLA means life and well-being.

The Hawaiianized-English form of ZOE is KOE, a native Hawaiian word which means surplus or excess.

Some Hawaiian Names for Pets, Boats and Houses

Very few animals were known to the ancient Hawaiians. They brought with them to the Islands on their voyaging canoes the pig (pua'a), the dog ('īlio), the rat ('iole), and the domestic chicken (moa). All except the rat, who came along as a stow-away, were raised for food.

Other animals, such as the cat, cow, goat, horse, and sheep first came to Hawai'i with the early European settlers.

The following list of pet names is comprised primarily of names we did not include on the 'people' list (since most people would not want to be named "Spot"!). However, many of the names on the 'people' list might also be appropriate for pets.

'Āhina	Gray
Aikāne	Friend
'Aikapa	A privileged friend who shares in the profits of a friend's land, sometimes sharing the work
Aka	Shadow
Ali'i	Chief
Auali'i	Royal, chiefly
'Auli'i	Dainty
'E'a	Dusty, also 'E'a'e'a
'E'elekoa	Stormy
'Ehu	Dusty, red-haired
'Ele'ele	Black
'Ele hiwa	Jet black
'Ele'ī	Blue-black
'Eleu	Active, alert, lively
'Eno	Wild, untamed, also 'Eno'eno

152

Halulu	Thunder
Hau-pūehuehu	Snowflake
Hekili	Thunder
Hihiu	Wild, untamed; also rare, uncommon
Hinahina	Gray
Hinuhinu	Glittering, as polished stones; bright shiny, splendid
Hiwa kea	Black and white; used to describe an all-black pig with white hoofs and white tips of tail, ears, and nose
Hiwa pa'a	Coal black; entirely black
Hōkū	Star
Holo nui	To run fast, to gallop
Honu	Turtle
I'a	Fish
Ihu-anu	Cold nose; name of a wind blowing down from the uplands of Kawela, O'ahu
Ikaika	Strong, powerful
'Īlio	Dog
'Iole	Rat
'Iole-lāpaki	Rabbit
'Iole-li'ili'i	Mouse
'Iole-pua'a	Guinea pig
Ka-hekili	The thunder
Ka-'imi	The seeker
Ka'inapu	Graceful, prancing motion
Ka-lā	The sunshine
Kama hele	Traveller
Ka-noa	The free one
Ka-nuha	The sulky one
Ka-pa'a	The firm, steadfast
Kāpi'i	Curly
Ka-puni	The favorite one
Kaupili	Beloved companion
Kei	One's pride and glory
Ke-kipi	The rebel

Ke-koa	The courageous one
Kiko	Spot
Kikokiko	Spotted, speckled
Koa	Brave, bold, fearless
Koke	Quick, swift runner
Koki	Snub-nosed, as a bulldog
Kolohe	Rascal, naughty
Komoiʻiʻi	Very small, tiny, of small stature; also said of people of little consequence
Konakona	Strong
Kōnunu	Rounded and well-shaped, as a lehua flower
Kūpaʻa	Loyal
Kupuʻeu	Rascal
Kū uaki	Sentinel, guardian
Kuʻu maka	Apple of my eye
Laeʻula	Well-trained, clever
Laka	Gentle, tame
Lālama	Daring, fearless, clever
Lālauahi	Gray, stormy-looking, smoke-colored
Lale	Legendery bird mentioned in old tales and songs as a sweet singer
Lapakū	Excessively active
Lelele	Frisky
Lelemu	Slowpoke, lazy
Liliʻi	Tiny
Lio	Horse
Mahamoe	Attractive, sleek, plump
Māhoa	To travel together in company; travelling companion
Maka	Favorite one
Mākaha	Fierce, savage, ferocious
Maka koa	Bold, fierce, unafraid
Maka launa	Friendly
Maka leʻa	Twinkle-eyed, mischievous
Makamae	Precious, highly prized

Makana	Gift, present, reward, prize
Makanahele	Wind, untamed; of the wilderness or forest
Makoa	Fearless, courageous
Malila	Ghostly, shadowy
Manu	Bird
Manu aloha	Love bird; the parrot, so called because it can extend greetings—aloha
Manu mele	Song bird
Ma'oha	Gray, gray-haired; cloud-capped mountains
Mea a'a	Adventurer
Mea nui	Beloved person or thing (sometimes said sarcastically)
Melemele	Yellow; also the name of a star
Miki	Quick, active, alert; also Mikimiki
Moa	Chicken
Moa-nui	Big chicken
Moelua	Striped
Mo'o	Lizard
Na'auao	Intelligent
Nahoa	Bold, defiant
Nākolo	Rumbling, roaring, as surf or thunder
Nanahea	Animated, as birds
Nani	Beauty
Nēnē hiwa	Prized, beloved, precious
Nīele	Busybody, inquisitive
Nohe'o	Mischievous, rascal
Nohonani	Sitting pretty
Nonolo	Purring
Nui	Large, big, great, important
Nuka	Large, plump, sleek
Nuku	Scolding, grumbling; also Nukunuku
'Oehu	Prancing, leaping

Ōhāhā	Flourishing, plump, healthy
'Ōheuheu	Fuzzy
'Ōhuluhulu	Shaggy
Ole	Fang
Olomea	Brown with darker stripes or spots
'Ōnēnē	Fussy
'Oni'o	Spotted, streaked with various colors
Palanehe	Noiseless, quiet, dainty
Pāne'ene'e	Slowpoke
Pano	Dark, deep blue-black; also Panopano
Pano pa'u	Glossy, glistening black
Pilialoha	Beloved companion
Pilikia	Trouble; also Pōpilikia
Pōhaka	Spot
Pōhina	Misty, gray, foggy, hazy
Poki	This is said to have been the name of Ka-mehameha the Great's favorite dog
Pōlani	Handsome, beautiful
Pōlehulehu	Twilight
Polo	Fatso; large, plump
Polo hana'ole	Fat one who does no work
Polohina	Misty, smoky, gray
Polohiwa	Dark, glistening black
Poloka	Frog
Pōlua	Dark, stormy
Pōlunu	Chubby, plump, short
Pōmaika'i	Lucky
Po'o hina	Gray-haired
Po'o kea	White-haired
Po'okela	Foremost, best, superior, champion
Po'o pa'a	Hard-headed, stubborn
Pōpō hau	Snowball
Pōpoki	Cat, said to be from the English words 'poor pussy'

Pōpoki pe'elua	Gray cat with darker markings, tabby cat Lit., caterpillar cat
Pua	Flower, blossom
Pua'a	Pig
Puahina	Gray
Puakea	Pale-colored, as a buckskin horse
Pualena	Yellow colored; lazy, layabout
Pūhuluhulu	Shaggy, downy
Pu'ipu'i	Plump, stout, stocky
Pū'uku'uku	Wee, tiny, small
Pu'u wai hao kila	Courageous, heart of steel
Uakea	Misty
Uauahi	Smoky
Uila, Uwila	Lightening
'Ula	Red, scarlet
'Umi'umi	Whiskers
Wahi nui	Big mouth, tattler

In ancient Hawai'i it was the prerogative of the high chiefs to name their houses and canoes. Pity the poor maka'ainana (commoner) who presumed to name his humble dwelling or canoe. Such presumption would certainly attract both the attention and wrath of the ali'i.

Today, even we maka'ainana can name our special possessions. The following lists, one for houses, and one for boats, offers just a few suggestions.

HOUSES
In Hawaiian house is HALE, and the house is KA HALE

Ala Hikiwale	Easy Street
Hālau-lani	High-born chief's large house
Halehale	High, towering, as a housetop or cliff
Hale-kū-lani	House befitting royalty
Hale-ka-mahina	House of the moon
Hale-lani	House of heaven
Hale Mōhalu	House of relaxation
Hale ola	House of life

157

Ho'okā'au'ana	Time spent pleasantly
Ho'o kipa	Welcome
Ho'o nanea	To pass the time in ease, peace, and pleasure
Ka-hale-wehi	The beautiful house
Kahua o Mali'o	Place of happiness, comfort, pleasure
Kaulana	Place of rest and quiet
Kaulana-mauna	Mountain resting place
Ka-lani-ehiku	Seventh heaven
Kau-noa	Place without kapu
Ke-'alohi-lani	The royal brightness, name of Queen Lili'u-o-ka-lani's seaside cottage
Kei	One's pride and glory
Kōaniani	Place cooled by a gentle breeze
Lālea	Bouy, beacon, a prominent object or landmark ashore to steer by
Luakaha	Enjoyable, pleasant, a place to which one is attached, a place for relaxation
Mamalu	Shady
Mili-lani	Beloved place of chiefs
Mōhalu	At ease, unrestrained
Lani-keha	Legendary part of heaven, frequent name for residences of high chiefs as that of Ka-mehameha III at Lā-hāina, Lit., lofty heaven
Nohonani	Sitting pretty
No ka'oi	Best of all
O'io'ina	Resting place for travellers
Pali-uli	A legendary land of plenty and joy said to be on Hawai'i
Pūnana	Nest, hive, Fig. home
Pu'u-hale	Hill house
Pu-uho'omaha	A resting place for travellers

Uluwehi	Lush and beautiful, a place where beautiful plants thrive

BOATS

'Au·i·ke·kai·loa	Travel in the distant seas
'Auli'i	Dainty, neat, trim, perfect
Hōkū 'ae'a	Wandering star
Holokai	Seafarer
Holopuni	To sail or travel around everywhere
'Īlio 'aukai	Sea dog, experienced sailor
Ka·'imi	The seeker
Kama hele	Traveller
Ka·noa	The free one
Ka·pa'a	The firm, steadfast
Kaukoe	To persevere in a straight course
Kei	One's pride and glory
Koa	Brave, fearless
Koloani	To go away silently
Kukua'au	To go smoothly
Ku'u maka	Apple of my eye
Lau hala lana	Vagabond, drifter
Mahoa	Travelling companion
Makahani	To skim lightly
Makakai	Sea-washed, spray
Mea 'a'a	Adventurer, valaint, intrepid
Niau	Moving smoothly, swiftly, silently, peacefully; flowing or sailing thus
Palanehe	Noiseless, quiet, dainty; to move in a dainty fashion
Po'okela	Foremost, superior, champion
Puni hele	Fond of going about from place to place; addicted to travel

8

Resources and Reading List

Ancient Hawaiian Civilization, a series of lectures delivered at the Kamehameha Schools, rev. ed., Rutland, Vermont, C.E. Tuttle Co., 1986.

Anderson, Christopher P. The Name Game. New York, Simon & Schuster, 1977.

Apple, Russ. "The Significance of Names," in Tales of Old Hawaii, Honolulu Star-Bulletin, 11-6-81.

Burlington, Scott, Instant Hawaiian, Kaneohe, Robert Boom Co., 1967.

Creamer, Beverly. "What's in a name?" in Honolulu Star-Bulletin, 5-26-76.

Churchill, William. Weather Words of Polynesia, Millwood, N.Y., Kraus Reprints, 1974.

Curious Keoki—What is your name in Hawaiian?, Hawaii State Library System, 1977.

Dunkling, Leslie. The Guinness Book of Names, Middlesex, England, Guinness Superlataives Ltd., 1983.

Elbert, Samuel H. and Mary K. Pukui. Hawaiian Grammar, Honolulu, University of Hawaii Press, 1979.

Elbert, Samuel H. Spoken Hawaiian. Honolulu, University of Hawaii Press, 1970.

Fields, Maxine. Baby Names from Around the World, New York Pocket Books, 1985.

Fornander, Abraham. "Hawaiian Names of Relationship, etc." in Thrum's Hawaiian Almanac and Annual, 1885.

Freidman, Favius. What's in a Name, New York, Scholastic Book Service, 1975.

Hawaii State Department of Health, Research and Statistics Office. "Babies Do Grow Up", revised 9-81.

Hawaiian Word Book. Honolulu, Bess Press, 1983.

Hyde, C.M. "Hawaiian Names of Relationships of Consanguinity and Affinity" in Thrum's Hawaiian Almanac and Annual, 1884.

Johnson, Rubellite K. and Mahelona, John K. Nā Inoa Hōkū, Honolulu, Topgallant Publishing Co., 1975.

Judd, Henry P. The Hawaiian Language, Honolulu, Hawaiian Services, 1939.

Kent, Harold Winfield. Treasury of Hawaiian Words. Honolulu, Masonic Public Library of Hawaii, 1986.

Kittelson, David. Hawaiianized English Given Names, Hawaii State Library System, 1973.

Krauss, Bob. "Person First in Hawaiian Name Giving", in Honolulu Advertiser, 10-24-73.

Lake, H. Keolamakaainana. "'Ohana, Love in a Song", unpublished, n.d.

Lydgate, John. "Hawaiian Personal Names" in Thrum's Hawaiian Almanac and Annual, 1917.

Mitchell, Donald D. Na Inoa Hawaii, unpublished, 1968.

Mitchell, Donald D. Resources Units in Hawaiian Culture, The Kamehameha Schools Press, 1982.

Murdoch, Clare G. Hawaiian Personal Names, Hawaii State Library System, n.d.

Nurnberg, Maxwell. What to Name Your Baby, New York, Collier, 1984.

Pukui, Mary K. and Elbert, Samuel H. Hawaiian English Dictionary, Honolulu, University of Hawaii Press, 1957.

Pukui, Mary K. and Elbert, Samuel H. Hawaiian Dictionary. Honolulu, University of Hawaii Press, 1971.

Pukui, Mary K. and Elbert, Samuel H. Hawaiian Dictionary, Honolulu, University of Hawaii Press, 1986.

Pukui, Mary K. Nānā i ke Kumu, volume 1. Honolulu, Hui Hanai, 1972.

Pukui, Mary K. ʻŌlelo noʻeau: Hawaiian Proverbs and Poetical Sayings, Honolulu, Bishop Museum Press, 1983.

Pukui, Mary K. Place Names of Hawaii, Honolulu, University of Hawaii Press, 1974.

Reinecke, John E. "Personal Names in Hawaii", in American Speech, no. 4, December 1940.

Ronck, Ronn. Ronck's Hawaiian Almanac. Honolulu, University of Hawaii Press, 1984.

Silva, Kalena and Kamanā, Kauanoe. The Hawaiian Language, its spelling and pronunciation. Honolulu, K. Silva, 1979.

Sleigh, Linwood and Johnson, Charles. The Book of Boy's Names, New York, Crowell, 1962.

Sleigh, Linwood and Johnson, Charles. The Book of Girl's Names, New York Crowell, 1962.

Taylor, Clarice B. with Pukui, Mary K. "Hawaiian Names", in Thrum's Hawaiian Almanac and Annual, 1948.

3,500 Names for a Baby. New York, Dell Publishing Co., 1969.

Train, John. Remarkable Names of Real People. New York, Clarkson N. Potter, 1977.

Wells, Evelyn. What to Name the Baby. Garden City, New York, Doubleday, 1946.